PARIS ART QUEST

by Lonnie Pelletier

Library and Archives Canada Cataloguing in Publication
Pelletier, Lonnie P., 1943
Title: Paris Art Quest
Cover by Lonnie P. Pelletier
Editing by Heidi Greco
Instar Publishing Inc
ISBN 978-1-928151-16-6
Subjects:
1. Pelletier, Lonnie P., 1943 - - Painter
2. History of modern painting.
3. Paris, France – - Art History

To my friends in Paris,
of so long ago.
We shared our youth and the
adventure of art, as our world
changed before us.

OTHER BOOKS BY LONNIE PELLETIER

*Art Quest
*Among Maya Ruins
* Galaxies - 65 Exoplanet Worlds
100 Travel Moments
Straw Man
Pelletier Chronicles - 500 Years
Anne And Jean
Sea Scout Sea
Life's Third Quarter

*In full colour (color)

PARIS ART QUEST CONTENTS

PART 1 THE JOURNEY OF YOUTH

Let me introduce myself. My name is Lonnie Paul Pelletier. Almost all of my friends and associates know me as Lon. I am a writer and a full time painter. Sometimes this is referred to as being an author and an artist – it's all a matter of perception. This may not be the only art book written in the first person, however it is one of the very few of them. I began this as a novel in 1966. I was attempting to communicate the importance of art as an evolution, and the book didn't look much like this. I've actually begun this book a number of other times. In my first attempts, I used the benchmark of well-known European paintings. When my resulting pages began to unfold as duplications of everything that I had previously read, I set that project aside.

My next attempts saw me using Canadian Art. Not only did many schools of artistic thought appear to be missing, many Canadian artists had simply followed their European counterparts with a lead-time of thirty years being lost in the process. As Canadian painters we are not necessarily imitators, but my project with its focus on the international art scene, made us look that way. Throughout this process of several attempts, I hadn't yet come to realize that what I was trying to say could be demonstrated with my own paintings. But at last, this idea took hold.

The fact that I am a Western Canadian will become obvious to the reader. Most of our traditional groups of painters have set the bar for Canadian Art as being evocative of Ontario or Quebec. We in Western Canada tend to be loners. Not only does our art reflect our individuality, but it also bears connotations of our rural nature. I have lived most of my adult life in Vancouver; my education in art took place primarily during my three years of study in Paris, France. However, it must be noted that our character is usually formed at a much younger age. I grew up in northern British Columbia and in central Alberta. Neither environment represented "big city living."

My best early memories are of a log cabin, on the edge of the Canadian Rockies where, for my first years of school, I lived with my maternal grandparents. I have numerous memories of that homestead, set in picturesque foothills, in front of the mountain that had been named by my grandmother. Her name for it was Sugarloaf Mountain, and the name stuck. It has always seemed to me that I was somehow blessed with the chance to experience what life must have been like in a previous century. The scenario was probably reminiscent of the mid-eighteen hundreds.

The cabin was a cozy home and was warmed by both a centrally located "potbellied stove" and by a wood-burning range. The floors were planks, which were always kept washed and clean. Beside the entry door was a wood box that stored the winter supply for the two stoves. At the time, the wood box seemed huge. When it was partially empty, I loved to play in it, and it became many wondrous things – a fort, a castle, a great outlaw's hideout – just about anything. The chunks of wood often became guns, cannons, or cars or trucks. Living there as the only child in this survival-geared environment, I could name all incidental pieces of wood, to be choices from the world as I then knew it.

Later, when I visited the cabin at about age seventeen, I was astounded by the size of this wood box. My formerly grandiose world comprised such small dimensions that I could only find it laughable. The real point of my log cabin illustration is not to compete with readers who may have grown up in similar circumstances, but to illustrate the fact that life is an adventure of learning, one that is both imaginative and figurative. In later years as I studied in art history courses in Paris, and literally found myself immersed in a curriculum spanning one thousand years, I realized that we all have to begin somewhere. Our mental destinations can complement our early background; they need not compete with it.

The result for me was that the more I studied art, the more I returned to nature. In the early sixties I thought that I could become an architect. But once I realized that it really wasn't the job that I wanted, I gave up that goal and bought a one-way ticket to Paris, France. Having worked hard, I'd saved enough money to not be immediately thrown into that newly named group of my peers called hippies, and set out to discover what I might really want to study. I knew that my desire was in the arts, but my interests were somewhere between Interior Design and the world of Dance.

At the time, such pursuits sounded rather effeminate, especially in that very red-necked part of the world. In fact, in Western Canada, the Arts section in the newspaper was generally called the "Women's Section". I was not effeminate; I am definitely heterosexual, but I did desire a life in the arts. Naturally, this was exactly why I was leaving. At that time in my life, I had worked primarily as a carpenter in construction, so I was used to being around people whose thought patterns were pretty much the opposite of mine.

It was one of the most astounding discoveries of my life when, at twenty-one years old, I stood before the great works of Cubism, Expressionism and Impressionism – and felt great emotion. Having read a number of books on art history, I was somewhat prepared for the intellectual wonders of that new world, but I had wrongly presumed that the process of understanding art was going to be one of technical memorization. However, the discovery that the subjects treated by my favourite artists were things I could identify with – and the fact that viewing their work resulted in "an evocation of a state of mind" – left me astounded.

After my first visits to the art museums of Paris, I realized that my world had just become much larger. I no longer worried about my "red-necked-but-close" friends back in rural Canada. At last, I had found my world. To this day I often enjoy visiting those first paintings that I viewed, as over the years, they have become my good friends. To this day I often also visit my "red-necked-but-close" friends. To my amazement, they have mellowed in their judgment of the arts world. Fortunately, the broader world has also changed.

Perhaps this is partly due to the hippie movement, which, like any movement, contained both good and bad. One of its broad-reaching effects was that individuality became acceptable. It managed to change a paradigm of bigotry and thought. In Canada, the arts became mainstream; as a result of this, it became acceptable for men to react emotionally to painting and literature. In the mid-Sixties I began my quest for material success. This meant I had to make some compromise - if I wished to work in the arts.

So I decided to become an art dealer. By working for three years, on a full time basis, as an international art dealer, and a total of fourteen more years part time, I established specific personal beliefs about the reality of art in the market place. Some very real reasons kept me from working at it full time. Mainly, my personal income goals could not be achieved from the process. My yearly income from the commercial world of art was never either constant nor completely satisfactory. Besides, I had decided early on, to never own an art gallery.

My observation of the marketing process at art galleries was that it was demeaning to everyone involved. Rather than describe the selling process within these writings, it may be adequate to state that my decision was based on both my academic background and my experience as a trainer of salespeople. The process of choosing an artwork can also be demeaning for the consumer. Often they are told by art dealers what they should like. In only a very few instances could it be successfully argued that a quick and judicious non-personal course might help them make better choices.

In any case, I preferred to sell at a corporate level, avoiding the façade of retail communication. My corporate dealings included working at the wholesale level in marketing directly to galleries. My first real insight about the art marketing scene came in the mid-Sixties. I realized that even though I had either sold or put on consignment nearly seventy-percent of the paintings displayed for sale in all of the art galleries in the cities of Edmonton and Calgary, the sales simply weren't happening. After a year, I still had an inventory available that I didn't want.

I saw that the art galleries stayed open only due to their cash flow from framing prints. Not willing to believe that the art scene was completely dead, I went on to other concepts. I mounted a series of large hotel exhibits in the five largest Western Canadian cities. By using combined banquet halls, I could always advertise that I was "exhibiting in excess of three hundred paintings." Using this process I was able to sell an average of one painting every half hour. Unfortunately, I saturated this specialized market within three years. It had quickly proven to attract a group of individuals who became loyal buyers at each exhibit, however each only wished a limited size of art collection.

Later, when other dealers tried to use the same methodology, but with mass-produced oil-on-canvas product, I set the concept aside. What did work was the process of selling directly to corporations. I produced and sent out catalogues, followed up with a phone call for an appointment – and sold five thousand and four paintings to one thousand and seven corporations in the space of approximately two years.

Many of the companies I dealt with preferred to lease before buying. The longest of these leases was for a group of twelve works that were leased for a total of eleven years – from 1973 to 1984. Just as I did with all the leases, I phoned at three-month intervals, on each billing date, and suggested that they buy the work outright. It was easy to realize from dealing with these leases that many corporations seemed to prefer to never have to make a decision on art.

Leasing allowed them to enjoy the works in their executive suites and offices without the potential embarrassment of a manager having to state that these were his or her personal choice. Purchasing outright would have represented a declaration of their artistic taste. There exists, even at the upper management level, the possibility of intimidation over going public with one's personal taste.

Once the eleven years expired, that particular firm simply asked me to pick up the paintings. They were now going to invest in interior design and wall reliefs in lieu of displaying art. I didn't really mind; the paintings had long since been well paid for. I can safely say that this process also enabled me to help establish a number of meaningful corporate art collections. It allowed me to work not only as a dealer, but also as a consultant.

Normally, I would buy the art outright and then sell it to the consumer. By working with an upper management group, or a person delegated as a liaison, I could buy on their behalf and thus create a more meaningful collection for them.

In the case of one large firm that had built ships since the mid-eighteen fifties, I was offered the loan of some of their old photographs. With the help of two other painters, we created new compositions by using details from those photographs. The firm was pleased enough with the results that they created a permanent display space for most of the oil paintings that resulted from our work.

Such was my world of Western Canadian corporate art. This was the same reality that had existed throughout history, where the artist requires a patron. In days of old that patron had been the church or the kings and queens of the day. My experience and study had led me to understand that the new patrons were the corporations

Other art dealers and artists have turned to government, by way of grants - as their patron. It's all just a matter of preference. Throughout this process of marketing, I remained a painter.

It may possibly seem to be a mercenary process, but I would like to draw a parallel to a professional musician. A musician will prefer a genre such as jazz, classical or country. Within that, he or she may prefer a style such as honky-tonk, punk or older rock-and-roll. While it is a given that a professional musician is capable of playing in all styles, it is understood that an amateur probably cannot. I believe that a similar truth applies to painting as an art form.

It is probably my European training that has made me biased in this respect. The traditional European process of learning to paint requires one to learn about many art movements. Then, only after completion of the accompanying academic studies, will the painter choose his or her favourite genre, and develop a personal style. This matter of style is something I had to deal with while I worked as an art dealer.

When I was handling the works of two hundred painters, I painted in the styles that were unavailable to me as a dealer. I simply "filled in" by painting works in styles that were not yet represented by the work of my clients, the artists.

I had advertised that all genres of painting were available through me. So, whenever I was presented with the opportunity to sell non-objective works, if I did not have a piece similar to the one requested, I would stand in as the artist. It was in this manner that during my "art dealer period," I sold over three hundred non-objective works of my own.

I should explain again that this was my personal form of compromise. Some of my associates taught art, and others purchased art galleries. In all of our cases, our first choice would have been simply to paint or sculpt. However, a common denominator existed. We had decided to have a family and preferred to raise our children in a style to which we wanted them to become accustomed. Being a starving artist wasn't among our goals.

I have had many teachers and my world of art allows me to reflect on many mentors. Like many individuals who have acquired training in Europe, I reflect not so much on the instruction doled out by my professors, but rather on what they taught me to see. Saying that we can be trained by the greats of art, merely from hours of museum observation, does injustice to the process. It was instruction by my art teachers that taught me how to view these works, and how to learn from them. Having said that, I can now state that the reason many of the definitions of art movements in this book are of a European nature is that these definitions are deduced from my mentors.

The excitement of sitting in a sidewalk café in Paris in the early sixties and discussing art until three in the morning gave me the feeling of being a part of a more vast world experience: As we discussed art and the reality of art, I was able to share the constant search for line with Tadao Sumikawa from Japan. We spoke of the relativity of the universe as shown in the outer space oils of Vila Monasterio from Spain. I learned about the relationship of texture and form found in the sand and-concrete works of Ebrin Adingra, an artist from the west coast of Africa. He had just won the first prize at the university. His frescoes had been recognized for the link they made between Cubism and the symbols of his former home in Africa.

I am proud of the fact that these were the people who became my friends in France. However dissimilar their former cultures may have been, their backgrounds were similar to mine.

We were not searching for any type of elite rather we were searching for the real. Later, as I met individuals who wished to use art pieces to flaunt their sense of elitism, I marveled at the irony. The culture consumers of our era can be just as removed from the reasons for art's existence, as were the former patrons in other periods of history. The city of Paris was also filled with young females, then my age, from every country imaginable. It was an exciting time to be young, open to new learning and willing to communicate with all other cultures.

I was able not only to spend the hundreds of hours of reflection before the masters of both antiquity and contemporary art, but I was able to have intelligent companionship by my side.

It would be a terrible understatement to simply say "all of this had created a new form of adventure for me." It was more than a new world – it was as if the planet had changed direction.

From my perspective, Western Canada was appearing to be anything but new. And now finally, almost forty years later, I have returned to the arts. While I was focused on commerce, and as long as my business administration credentials were being used, I felt that I wasn't really involved in the arts. But now my children had not only become adults, they had even completed their desired academic pursuits. Throughout their growing up, I had continuously reminded them that they should pursue those occupations that would fulfill their own passions. Now, as they reached their twenties, they kept reminding me that it was my turn to do the same. They said that my passions should become relevant again. I finally left marketing entirely and became completely immersed in writing novels, composing music – and most importantly – in painting.

I hope that I am able to communicate that the process of learning about art, and the process of attempting to find the right line, colour or texture. My greatest wish is to pass along the ability to look at and see art works. Though I realize that most of my readers may already have this skill, I know that learning to see was the principal lesson I learned from my early European experience. Over the last few years I have returned to Europe to experienced a reunion with some of my old friends – the great paintings.

PART 2 THE PARIS OF EXPERIENCE

Sandwich Jambon (ham) was still the cheapest item on the menu, and it was still less than the price of a pint of beer. In a world of much change, the basics of French tourism had remained constant. On this, my second day back in Paris, I felt very much assured that I had somehow arrived back at my second home. Home is a place that's stable and familiar, with consistent patterns of behaviour, and all of this about me, I felt, defined home. My third day was a nostalgic walking tour past classrooms and sidewalk cafés, places I'd known forty years ago, so this was a thoughtful time, with much reflection. I intended to have a drink at what had been one of my favourite cafés on the Left Bank. But to my surprise, the place had been transformed into a very large sushi bar. I walked past it, heading for a second favourite site.

In the sixties, I had obtained two postcards that pictured two alternate scenes of the corner at Boulevard Saint Michel looking up Rue Soufflo towards the Pantheon. One had been taken during the then new age of photography (almost one hundred years prior), and as a black and white photo, it showed the two corner sidewalk cafés fronted with horse drawn carriages. The second coloured postcard showed the same corner cafés – with even the same canopies – but with efficient nineteen sixties European cars quickly passing.

In March of 2005, I had returned to the Paris that I had remembered. After picking up my apartment keys, I headed for the tunnels of the Metro. The smell of it washed over me like a tidal wave in slow motion. Any underground system will sustain an environment, and the Paris Metro was no different. This smell wasn't a stench. It was something in the air that felt like warm welcome. At the point of being enveloped in the scented cloud of evocative memory, I felt a specific emotion. It was a sense of fulfillment that came with my realization that – after four decades of staying away, I really was back in the city I loved – Paris.

Spending the next two days just settling into my apartment was a treat. I took my time getting organized, as I wanted to feel part of the neighbourhood. This was not the tourist's Paris, and I was enjoying it. "In France, the tip is included in the bill," the waiter insisted. I had forgotten. After a two-hour walk, in a circle around the area of my new home, I had finally sat down. My initial observations indicated that there had not been a change in forty years – at least not in neighbourhoods like this one.

Mine was the twentieth district and it seemed to have remained intact. French beer was still less in price than imported. All beer was close, or even less in price, than lemonade or a small glass of Coke. Eleven postcards depicted two worlds, over fifty years apart, where not even two World Wars raging through Paris had changed these two cafés and their social ambience.

On this visit however, the cafés revealed themselves as not entirely impervious to the realities of the world. One was now a fast-food pizza place, and the other sported the tacky golden arches of McDonald's. I forced a French thought, as I stood in amazement, and shook my head - *C'est la vie*! I made the decision that there would be nothing nostalgic about having anything in either a sushi café or a McDonald's, and I continued on my walking tour towards other, more authentic Parisian delights. I didn't allow myself to feel personally slighted.

I reminded myself of the cliché, that one can never go back. The crowded streets, so full of students who looked so very young, reminded me that last time here, I must have been much younger too.

Day four, my second trip to the Left Bank, was more fruitful and was less of a shock. I remembered that it had often been written that there were many different dimensions of Paris. The businessman's Paris was different from the sailor's Paris.The fashion industry's Paris did not interact with the tourist's Paris. The students' Paris did, at one time, coincide with the Paris of intellectuals. It was now obvious that the Left Bank of students and intellectuals had both physically – and spiritually – been taken over by tourism. What I was experiencing within my observation was that change. Nothing that I had hoped to revisit coincided with this tourist's version of Paris.

I felt sorry for the students who I couldn't help observing, as they tried their best to "put up" with the massive façade of all these tourists so intent on "experiencing the Left Bank". I also felt sorry for the tourists, as the Left Bank and all that it represented (especially, intellectually) no longer existed. The culture of McDonald's really had taken over.

Members of the intelligentsia may still be the normal ruling body behind the walls of the Sorbonne. I hoped so; however, I decided to leave any analysis to my observations of the physical life of the Left Bank. I knew that I probably would never visit it again.

Place du Tertre and Montmartre were now places that offered only souvenirs – both in the sense of trinkets, and in the richer, French-language meaning of memories. Even in "my day" of forty years prior, the area had been transitional. The Impressionist painters and the writers of the area, with their having chosen these other *digs* and surroundings other than the Left Bank – had then again left.

Even in the sixties, before, many art galleries of substance had thrived here, but now they lived only in memory. The few remaining galleries had added lesser-priced items to their stock in order to survive the "quick-serve" tourists with their two and three-day itineraries. Seeing the Paris of business next, gave me hope. It had become a city of scattered highrise buildings, and was linked to the rest of the world of commerce. The "purists", as lovers of the original and traditional Parisian beauty, hated the new look; however, the buildings had substance. They seemed as tangible as the Paris intellectual groups had been in the past.

They also reminded me that as a Canadian, I was part of the continent that that had replaced the traditional. As a centre of the world of art and architecture, the original Paris no longer existed. Just as distributed database technology and information systems had replaced central mainframe computers, world creativity was now dispersed throughout a widely disseminated system. The new paradigm was not one of leadership and acceptance by an elite creative community in Paris, as it had been in the past. It was now global.

Within my excitement of visiting the Centre Georges Pompidou for the first time, I was reminded that I had acquired an incredible training in Art History in this city. A great deal of my knowledge had been accumulated here, and it is to Paris and its museums that I give all credit. In Paris the building of the Georges Pompidou National Centre of Art and Culture is considered the epitome of revolutionary avantgarde styling. The Museum of Modern Art is on the third and fourth floors and is possibly the largest, or at least one of the largest in the world. For me viewing the quality was important. The Centre is also put forth as providing ongoing forums for debate and intellectual exchange.

I suspect it does very well at replacing both the "Left Bank" and the "Montmartre" intellectual and social concepts of old. As I compared, my personal interpretation of Jackson Pollack's style seemed to possibly be the exception – one thing I had learned elsewhere. I needed to have more confidence in respect to the styles of Vlaminck, Matisse and Leger. Using specific strokes, which I later observed in the Picasso Museum, I knew I could now be comfortable with myself in the context of my work. I had not left any use of style behind.

My works had now included much that I was seeing including the vitality of Mondrian. As a colourist I felt that I was one of "them." Such is the ego of an artist - without that ego, accomplishments in art would not exist. I was viewing the "greats" of my world. However, culture and influence may take side roads and odd journeys. After the last paintings of the 1950's I could no longer relate to French influence. Still, I am sure this was a positive step in my thought process. It meant that, as related to truly contemporary art, I had become myself. I was not simply influenced by the France of one hundred years ago, nor was I later just following Northern European trends, even though this would have been perfectly normal.

I went beyond simply finding New York modern schools of artistic thought to be valid, on to yet another usual part of twentieth century artistic thought. I suspected that, in art, I had somehow become Canadian – and that this wasn't a negative, but a positive idea. It was here and now at this museum that I was able to ascertain these very positive differences.

Fortunately, I did not suffer much shock at the changes that had taken place in the *Les Halles* District, where The Centre had been built. Old Paris used to have one of the largest farmer's markets in the world, and this had been its location. Along with the number of huge agricultural distribution warehouses was the Parisian lifestyle that went with the market. In many of the small second floor restaurants near this fresh food supply in this very large city, it was considered fashionable to dine at three o'clock in the morning. For students and artists it was not only fashionable but simply logical to dine here, on inexpensive but delicious fresh sausage, or huge servings of fish and fried potatoes. I had eaten there many times.

Les Halles was also known for the beautiful farmer's daughters who would accompany the produce brought in by their families. Unfortunately, some of the more decadent "families" supplied them as prostitutes, and these young women could be found sitting for display on the numerous rooming house staircases throughout the Les Halles area. I remembered that when I'd been a student, walking by with my friends, we had seen these girls and realized that they were our age. We'd both identified with them, and felt very sorry for their plight. While we knew that education was not accessible to everyone then, we had hoped that the world would soon change for these girls.

I was happy to see that it had. I also knew that most tourists would never realize that the large footprint of the Centre Georges Pompidou had replaced a very negative man made system that had been decades old. I marvelled at the multitude of new shops selling CD's, tourist trinkets and the many contemporary versions of the fried potatoes and sausage. Les Halles as I remembered it, had been entirely replaced. It was now just the name of a bus and subway stop – a name used in popular fiction, about some other time.

My solitary walk crisscrossing the new area was very enjoyable. As in many such ventures, even in Paris there is no real sadness relating to change. At the Picasso Museum I had observed another type of nostalgia. It had to do with picture frames. Determining where and how best to present, and preserve, a work of art – how to make it sing in its new surroundings – is one of the pleasures of art ownership. This responsibility is left to the consumer as the owner of the work. I began to notice a specifically European style of presentation. Europe's rich past will always have an influence on interior design there, especially in France.

Picasso's works from the 1930's were being presented in the bold and even aggressive designs of early seventeenth century Spanish frames. His analytical cubism was presented in seventeenth century Italian gilded frames. The result of such presentation was unmistakable as a positive metamorphosis involving the total art form. However, the trend for white box frames around contemporary art will – and probably should, continue - because the painting as art must live its own life, not as merely a decorative piece. It is in choice of frame that an owner's cultural influence or background is the ruling factor. A frame that is baroque in design, as used by a European, has a different connotation than it would in a newer culture, like North America's. In the wrong context, the antiquated frames become an exaggerated juxtaposition of traditional and modern. Although such a contrast may occasionally "work," most often it is just quirky, as it seems mostly a presentation of the unexpected. Degas was using painted white frames in the 1880's - for exactly those reasons. On other occasions, as a North American, I had felt uncomfortable with the exaggerated contrast of nostalgia in frames.

It seemed fitting that I would now visit Place du Tertre for a second time. When I'd been here forty years earlier, some quality of art as a creative process had existed in this square. Without the Sunday explosion of tourists, I thought that perhaps I could view art – rather than the slew of terrible paintings I had quickly critiqued on the first visit. Unfortunately tourist "schlock" now completely dominated these oil painting presentations. The number of painters around the square had not varied over half a century. The styles were also of a certain pattern. About a dozen painters did small street scenes and floral works, in vivid colours, designed to sell. I could only compare their works to mass-produced ashtrays. Another dozen painters did larger street scenes. These were of a slightly better quality, and I'm sure, would find their way onto the walls and into the living rooms of these many frantic consumers.

The Paris street scenes had evolved to being pastel in colour, rather than the darker browns with dashes of primary reds and yellows of previous decades. As always, in evaluating the total group, between two and four painters could actually paint. It would be obvious to those who knew art that this smaller group probably painted elsewhere –and, as I suspected, would then probably paint under a different name, likely their own. Such was the case of Villa Monasterio, someone I had known in my earlier Paris years. He would paint scenes of wrinkled old men with glowing pipes. Now, two other artists had replaced him with the same (obviously "marketable") style. Villa had always signed his Place du Tertre works with only his first name. He knew, as we all knew, that no other successful game existed for street painters. Each painter could sell two-dozen "works" per month. This represented a steady income. But even in the sixties, Villa signed his "real" art works with his last name. It was by these more serious works that I was influenced to paint outer space.

As an art dealer, I had purchased and sold over fifty of his best works. I had sold these "Monasterios" in Western Canada for up to five thousand dollars. Even adjusting for inflation, it clearly was a successful venture in art for both of us. In 1974 I had given Villa a guarantee of one thousand dollars per month. For that I was to receive a minimum of three works per pay period. We carried on with this plan for six months, by which time Villa had achieved his financial goal of being able to return to Spain with its much warmer climate. He had consistently complained during winter months in Paris that he was freezing.

The second artist I dealt with was Ebrin Adingra. Originally from what used to be called the Ivory Coast, Ebrin had won the "First Prize of the Beaux-Arts of Paris". In winning this very prestigious award, Ebrin had shown himself to be more than just a promising young artist. The historic liaison between African works, which had evolved into Cubism, had never been better portrayed. Working on a sand laden canvas, he produced a rock-relief look that was very popular. Both he and Villa had far surpassed Place du Tertre levels of art. They were just two examples supporting my theory that a small minority existed among this larger group who were capable of excelling in art.

On my second visit to the Place du Tertre, I felt that I might never come back. If I were going to ask about my former associates, I knew this had to be the time. I had purposely returned on a weekday so that the numbers of tourists would be down. The Place du Tertre of today is like a country fair. It is a rectangular open space that is surrounded by small cafés and (now) larger restaurants. It could be described as a marketing zoo. It is through a process of bartering and negotiating in many languages, that hundreds of not very creative works are sold every week. In my past and also as an art dealer, I used to visit just to observe. Despite the way so many of these paintings had been unsophisticated, I knew that most art galleries needed to learn that there was something here that was working. I hated this system and the fact that so many "things" that were just so much oil on canvas were selling under the guise of being art. However, I knew that it provided a cash flow to the painters, which enabled them to paint more seriously elsewhere.

I had once been one of those painters. I approached a gentleman standing behind his easel as he was about the same age as me – and also was painting a landscape that in fact was not that bad.

We spoke in French. "Pardon me, I used to paint here some forty years ago – and I would like to inquire about a couple of my friends who were here also."

"Yes, of course." He didn't seem irritated by my asking for free information.

"Two of my friends here were Villa Monasterio and Ebrin Adingra."

"When did you say they painted here?"

"Thirty to forty years ago." Because of his age, my statement did not seem ridiculous.

"I've only been here about twenty years, but I think that I know Adingra. Was he a black man?"

"Yes. He painted in sand." I stated this as Ebrin almost seemed to be the only person in the world who painted in sand. That isn't really the case, but with his tremendous originality of style, Ebrin had captured an ownership of sand painting.

The man motioned to the nearby corner easel. "The lady sitting over there would know. She is the "Grande Dame" of Place du Tertre. She knows everyone that has ever painted here. Come, I'll give you an introduction."

I followed him over to two women who were sitting comfortably behind their paintings. Each was looking past their work in order to catch the eye of any tourist who might be contemplating a purchase.

"Madame, I would like to introduce a painter from the past. He wishes to inquire about two of his friends who used to work here." He was introducing me with the flair of a presentation to royalty.

I stepped forward and interjected quickly, being as informal as I could, in an attempt to bring a more normal flow to our communication.

"Yes, excuse me, but I used to paint here almost forty years ago, and I had friends I would like to inquire about."

Without hesitation she made a statement that completely threw me off guard. "I remember you. You were a Canadian."

I looked at her more thoroughly. I also could now remember her. The sixties and seventies were all about looking cool – especially in Paris. And now I was remembering her – not as this elderly, grey-haired lady before me, but as a young and vibrant girl. She had been very stylish dressed for that era and she always enjoyed the company of her "fellow" painters. I also remembered speaking to her in some of the following years, in my role as an art dealer. During that period, I had diplomatically explained to her that commercial work such as hers could not be purchased and sold within my process. More specifically, her oil paintings – of flowers on canvas – were definitely not art.

"Who are you wondering about?" As she spoke, it was as if years had disappeared between us and we were simply continuing a former conversation.

"Villa Monasterio and Ebrin Adingra. I had other friends, but I've forgotten their names."

"Ebrin died just last week! He is dead." She stated this in such a matter of fact way that it shocked me.

The woman beside her spoke up. "He died of cancer – last week - finally."

I managed to stumble out a phrase or two. French is my second language and with the shock of coincidence,

I was not thinking quickly. The coincidence that shocked me was two fold. Firstly, I had just missed meeting him again after all of these years, and secondly, he had once again been painting at Place du Tertre, like in the old days.

Rose, the first woman I'd spoken to, now explained, "He had been sick for a year and he hadn't painted here since last spring."

"Did he still paint with sand?" I remained at a loss for words, but then added, "He had such a great style."

Rose knew what I was asking. "Yes, he never changed that style in all of those years. Each composition was different though. Sometimes he changed colours – mostly to amuse himself. But he never changed."

All of a sudden, it was as if I was at a social event and I wanted to be extra complimentary. "His style was very contemporary. I really liked his work. I still hang his paintings in my home."

"What was your other friend's name?" The second woman asked. I repeated it, adding that he painted outer space, and that for those works he used his last name. I observed them both, as that fact seemed to trigger some memories.

Rose remembered it all. I was trying to remember if she had been Villa's girl friend, but the detail wouldn't come back. She seemed to concentrate, then she replied, "Villa Monasterio went back to Spain about that time. He has never returned – never."

"He was Basque." I stated this, if only to reassure her of my former friendship with him.

"Yes, and you had another friend here – another Canadian. He painted large street scenes. He liked the large canvases."

"Yes, I smiled widely." We were reliving our youth.

The second woman sat up straighter. "There are no other painters left from then. Only about four or five of us – from the entire group! About thirty died of cancer. Do you understand – cancer?"

I knew she was asking something more, but I kept my reply simple. "Yes, I understand it well."

Both women had customers waiting. Their small calendar art paintings were selling at four times the price of similar works in Canada, and I knew from experience that they could not afford to keep their customers waiting. I stepped back politely and waited. One of them concluded a successful sale of two works, but the other didn't. We then visited again briefly.

Rose's friend was specific. "The painters from Poland used to be here. Many good artists were here. No one comes from behind the old Iron Curtain anymore. But I remember - you all painted such big works – huge works. Now only souvenirs are to be found here. There are only terrible tourist works now. Do you remember those times?"

I smiled and I paused and remembered. I also remembered meeting Rose at the café that used to be small. It was on the corner of Place du Tertre, only a few metres from us. Like most businesses here, it had now been enlarged to encompass the two adjoining shops. I could see the white table clothes as the symbol of the much more formal place that it had become.

Rose had reminded me of it. "You and your friend always had a beer on the corner here. It was a hangout for painters then. We all painted."

I also remembered why her memory was specific. When I met her she was the girlfriend of one of the painters. I still couldn't remember his name, though I knew it didn't matter. I did recollect that he was a very sarcastic fellow and he was probably hard to get along with. What I remembered about her was that she was pretty. We'd had a series of those meetings we sometimes experience in life, where potential couples meet, while being involved with someone else. I was thinking of how two people can both know that they are interested in each other, but understand that the timing is wrong. I'm sure we were both remembering those far off days in the same way. I felt that it was better to leave things the way they were. It had been another time and another place. I smiled at this now-elderly lady and I said my good-byes. This was with the knowledge that even though my stay in Paris would last another two months, I would not visit them again. The art world of Europe has a hierarchy and they would feel very uncomfortable talking to me, and I to them. They would now consider me an academician and someone who never had to withstand the harsh elements in order to make a living. Even as I had replied to their inquiry of whether life had been successful for me in Canada over the years, I had purposely diminished my statement of that success.

As I then strolled down the streets of Montmartre while being deep within my thoughts, I compared our visit to one that might have taken place at a high school reunion. Our conversation may have been superficial, but it held much meaning for all of us. Those two women and Ebrin Adingra had painted there for the last forty years. That thought made my mind spin. For the two women, and their style of work, it likely seemed a way of life to be expected. Yet I couldn't feel sorry for Ebrin. He had a family of six children. Now he had passed away, leaving probably a large and wonderful family. He had told me about his earlier life, growing up in the tribal warfare of rural Africa. I knew of the hut where he'd been born. Paris had given him what he had desired in life. Reflection on success seems in order at the news of anyone's death. He would have painted a minimum of one hundred works per year. Four to five thousand "Ebrin Adingra"s were now hanging in homes, offices and galleries around the world. There is justice and honour, in spite of a lifetime of condescending responses from tourists, and standing in the bitterly cold winter rains of Place du Tertre – all the while painting and selling, selling and painting.

We had been there just after the time of great and well known street painters. It had been Utrello's paintings of the street scenes of Place du Tertre, which had made it so well known. And his works could now only be seen in the best of museums. In my contemplation, I wished that I could visit Villa Monasterio; such is the essence of friendships from the past.

The next days would take me back to the history of Paris, however this visit made me feel that in some very small way, I myself was now a part of it. I was able to visit some other old friends at the Orsay Museum. The old paintings of the Masters have always been friends to many. They speak to us in a natural way. As communication they have been very successful. It also seemed almost eerie.

The works I now thought of as "old" were from merely twice the time span, back to the period of my having painted in Paris. I'd lived in Paris forty years ago, yet many of the Post-Impressionist works were from as recently as only eighty years ago. This is something most of us never think of in our youth – the way we also become a part of history through life's adventure.

As I toured the museums, I followed the development of painting in a chronological order. Like so many other painters, for most of my life, I'd said that my best training was from contemplation before the work of the Masters. Now after so many years of painting, revisiting my "School of the Masters" revealed even more detail to me. In *La Falaise d'Etretat après l'ouage*, Gustave Courbet had used a particular style to paint rocks, foliage and grass, and even ocean. I understood that I had emulated it over the years. To my amazement I had been painting both trees and soil in the style of Pissaro, as shown in many of his paintings throughout the early 1900's. I had also learned from Paul Cézanne. In La Maison du pendu Auvers sur-oise that he painted in 1873, I had used the same methodology of painting rock facing. My roof texture was also often the same as in this earlier work of his. I had learned composition from Renoir. However, I knew I could never be the colourist that he was. I had painted the water of seascapes in the manner of Boudin from 1894, and snow in the manner of Sisley in his 1875 painting of La neige à Marly-le-Roi. My seascape from Holland had replicated the moon by Manet from Claire de Lune sur le port de Boulogne, painted in 1869. Mine were not copies, but they indicated a learned mannerism and technique.

I was not a "great," but I was a dutiful student. In most cases, I had long forgotten the source from which my technique had evolved. Like other painters all around the world, we had learned before these works and had then returned to our homelands, inspired. Other individuals have compared my seascape's blues to the emotion of the blues used by Van Gogh. I always thought that critique to be very naïve. My respect for Van Gogh had more to do with the fact that his works were simply my favourite. When I observed that in fact I had emulated his use of darker blues, I experienced a different emotion – one of feeling very humble. This emotion came from the fact that it seemed almost blasphemous on my part to even compare any aspect of my own works to his.

My trees and grass had been conditioned by Monet from his painting of *Effet de Vent*, one of his 1891 works. But the most important realization came to me when I stood before the four paintings of *Cathedrale de Rouen*. As for the technique, I now finally understood the processes and methods the style involved. I knew that under-painting was everything when it came to that which we see. In essence, this was the main course of the meal. Using this analogy, the topical painting (that which is viewed as predominate), being the final touch by the artist, could be compared to being the dessert. That final understanding was as important to me as the ability to replicate the other techniques in my own minor way.

While I was writing this, I was completing another book, a novel called *Pelletier Chronicles - 500 Years*. In it, I had attempted to describe some of the horrors of living in the Middle Ages. On this museum visit I found the ultimate evocation. In *Scène de guerre au Moyen Age*, by Edgar Degas (done in 1865) the reality of the Middle Ages is portrayed. Four nude female corpses lie on the ground; with one being trampled by a horse and rider. Four other women stand in various postures of nudity showing their helplessness, while a man on a horse aims his bow and arrow at them. They have no protection whatsoever. The three horses are huge and aggressive, as compared to the frail bodies of the women. The horses seem to be protecting the men as one of them carries loot, and another carries his choice of a woman like a sack. This was truly evocative of the essence of control by the haves over the have-nots. During that era, "knights" in armour consistently carried off whatever they desired from village and rural people. Only a painting could really illustrate that level of helplessness within a system.

Later, I would make a reference to it in my novel as it helped evoke the realities of the sixteenth and seventeenth centuries. On a later visit to the Louvre, I discovered a work called *Pillage d'un Village*, painted by Sébastian Vranck in 1589, which I found to be just as specific. It showed armed men on horses killing both female and male villagers. The unarmed were pleading for their lives, but to no avail. Clothing was already being torn off the dead bodies as loot. Many of the trees depicted were dead – symbols of the vanity of the knights and of death itself.

Not that many feet away, Ruben's painting, *Un Tourno*i, was hanging. Even though it was of the same approximate period, it glorified the allure of knights in shining armour, and showed them sparring against each other, as if they were evenly matched, and with all the mannerisms of great chivalry.

Communication in art is like that – the choice of message is up to the individual painter. The Louvre is unquestionably one of the most prestigious museums in the world. It is now also the most popular. It is a magnificent building, originally constructed in the 1200's as a fortress, and it would later become a royal palace of great magnitude. The ensuing construction took place over a period of seven hundred years. Its collection is broken into eight main divisions: Oriental Antiquities; Egyptian Antiquities; Greek, Etruscan and Roman Antiquities; Paintings; Sculptures; Objets d'art; Arts of Islam; Prints and Drawings; as well as presentations which cover The History of the Louvre and The Medieval Louvre. To this are added exhibitions that are temporary. The Paintings are well divided into five categories, with drawings included. They are French Paintings; Prints and

French Drawings; German, Flemish and Dutch Paintings; German, Flemish and Dutch Drawings; and German, Flemish, Dutch, Belgian, Russian, Swiss and Scandinavian Paintings.

Much of what I perceive about the history of the world comes from the many hours I spent in the Louvre. I am sure that the many weeks and months I passed there during my young twenties have had a tremendous effect on my life. Those changes that took place in my youthful thinking are not something that I will ever be able to properly measure. Experiencing the new Paris and the *Cité de la Musique* reminded me of my youthful transition from being a rather naïve prairie boy to someone completely immersed in music history. Music – especially my experience of it during the sixties in Paris – had broadened my youthful worldview.

Visiting now brought back so much. This new permanent venue is a place of much exchange. It fosters access to culture through concerts, museums and exhibitions, and it reminded me how much of a young person's experience studying in Europe, is about experiencing the history of Europe. It is the academic repertory, addressing all periods from the Middle Ages to the present. This includes modes of expression such as jazz or popular music. For most of us who went through this type of learning process, it was difficult to explain upon our return to North America; it just became one of those non-tangible personal assets.

The Folies-Bergère, where I had worked part-time as a student in the sixties, was now closed with boarded windows. It had existed as a Music Hall since 1869. Where its only importance to me was as a measuring point for calibrating my former Paris, I found its closing more a statement about the change in nightlife, in what used to seem to me to be a very vast community. It was not that anyone would have classified it as representing the fine arts, but it was very much live art. Most of the small live performance venues around the city had also closed their doors and it was an indication of the trend.

Relative to painting, there are many art exhibitions in Paris that are peripheral to the museum system. The federal government administers one system, parallel to that of the many municipal governments. Each has their ongoing permanent displays, and from these are drawn exhibitions designed to forever capture the imagination of the public. Art is kept alive by the sorting and resorting of the same paintings, all to be exhibited under different banners in varying presentations.

Upon observing Monet's work at the Musée Marmottan I made some simple notes to myself: "Do a self-portrait showing more unpainted canvas such as Monet did." In his Impressionism *Soleil Levant* of 1873 he painted almost in a monochrome of blue, with the orange sun reflection being so magnificent due to the use of little conflict of other colour. I have also never seen anything float in the manner of the subjects of Monet. I noted that I needed to use blurred outlines on water, and dark over light, in his manner, in order to achieve that unique floating effect on water. In my notes, I wrote: "Use more pink in my clouds." I left his display feeling that I had a lot of work to do. Such is art. A style is never complete. Art is always a personal evolution. I also believe that Minimalist styles in art were very much refreshed and influenced by him. He said so much, while painting so little – as no one else could, or even now can do.

The *Marmotttan Musée* was the nicely restored townhouse of Claude Monet and his friends and it is named after the Marmottan family who made it their home. The main floor holds paintings, tapestries, sculptures and furnishings from the 18th century. Upstairs paintings were by Monet, Sisley, Pisarro, Renoir and Morisot. However it is at the basement level where the prized Monet Gallery exists. It is here where the Monet water lilies are hung, with their shades of purple and orchid unlike any colour in the world of art. While here I found it difficult to know how long I should stay. There is simply no logic when it comes to deciding how long might be logical to contemplate such paintings. Nonetheless, I observed and humbly made notes. In the end, it seems I stayed a few hours. The works of Gustave Moreau, a symbolist of the same period as Monet, reminded me of a number of issues in art. The first is obvious to any viewer of his monumental works: because he didn't need to sell his works, he failed to complete many of them. But the second issue is more important. It is impossible to contemplate his work without realizing the number of painters that he influenced.

The black linear forms of Matisse, the sketch views of Picasso, the harsh colours of Van Gogh – all are a part of his presentation and style. He did not have the same goals as they did, however, with much of his style, he was the first and they followed. It was in the context of seeing these masters imitating other masters, that I saw how learning from each other's works was indeed the ideal. I felt that I could actually be one of that creative assembly of artists. I didn't mean this as any ego-driven assumption of quality, but I believed that learning their methodologies would benefit my personal advancement. The process of simulation of style could help me progress in my own artistic achievements.

Gustave Moreau's former home is now a National Museum, a step above a local municipal one. Within the hierarchy of Paris this fact is significant. Often listed as a forerunner of the Fauvist style, he also influenced Redon, Picasso and Dali. Like the later Surrealists, there is mysticism and fantasy in every canvas.

Touring back on the Left Bank I finally discovered yet another unchanged building, at 4 rue Saint Julien Le Pauvre. Amazingly intact, the Hotel Esmeralda was still the least expensive hotel on the Left Bank. Its ancient, low, dark oak-beamed ceiling gave me a minor sprinkling of my past. I had once lived there for five months. The Medieval look of the quaint lobby had no comparison - then or now. It was directly across from the Notre Dame Cathedral's anthropology museum and I had walked over from it, upon looking over and recognizing one of my old "haunts". As a hotel, it had a wonderfully traditional Parisian look. The sidewalk café one very short block away was still very much in business.

If I desired, I could have booked a room in the hotel, and then sat and had a beer in "my old café", while maybe even forgetting that forty years had passed. I paused on the street for reflection. My rented apartment was more to my liking – and the café was solidly packed from wall-to-wall with tourists. "Maybe next time", I thought.

Having immersed myself in the history of war from the Middle Ages to the present – at the Army Museum – I was able to make the mental transition back to 1900 by spending the rest of the day just across the street in the beautiful gardens and the Museum of Auguste Rodin. The quiet beauty of Rodin's work was an extreme contrast to the armoury of war. Both were very relevant to my research as a writer. However, the word research can be misleading. It is really the experience of the ambiance of the museum, set in a period of time, that transcends, as related to a written novel or document.

Later within the same week, I was able to observe that a specific presentation was being made in the "Musée national de la Marine". The grandeur of Napoleon and other early rulers was well demonstrated throughout the museum in both paintings and artefacts. Many models of ships from the previous four hundred years were also displayed. All were showing the grandeur of the time.

It wasn't until 1857 that Jean-François Millet painted *L'Angélus du soir* and *Des Glaneuies*. Only then did French culture finally refer to the emotions and intelligence of rural farm workers. The Barbizon School of Painting, which evoked the state of mind of rural and trades people, had not yet had an impact on seascapes. There were some larger seascape works by Joseph Vernet, who in pre-revolutionary France had been called "The Painter to the King". As I had earlier observed, these paintings from the 1700's, presenting the court of kings, were of a biased mentality. The dates of the paintings correlated to and confirmed my observation of non-democratic tendencies and elitism in the art of this period. It began to appear as if the paintings of lesser sea scenes had never been done in any significant number. I knew that they existed, but they were simply not presented at this museum – as if they were irrelevant.

Specifically I began to look for any type of replication of the cargo vessels that had transported so many immigrants from France to countries all around the world. Such was the evolution of art in France. It was no coincidence that Canadian History, and our culture, had shown a more democratic face to the men of the sea. With this in mind, there could still be a learning process for my own technical understanding. This visit was not without my usual notes.

"All halyards are astern of masts.

All stern cabins both with and without balconies cantilever out at the sides.

The French war ships of 1850 to 1900 were metal on wood and were never built without a type of battering ram bow."

No museum trip should be devoid of learning and I felt like I was still a novice in historic maritime art.

I also made a note of a 1627 painting by Claude Vignon, The *Claude de Razilly Allegory*, the only painting I knew of representing the 1641 immigration of my family, but one which led to my subsequent replication of ships of the period and type.

I left my next re-visit to the Louvre for last. Even though many "side" exhibitions were included during this stay in Paris, I had now visited all of the main art museums. Even though the Louvre had been the mainstay of my more "formal" education in Paris, in reality my time there had not followed any formal curriculum at all. What had made it seem formal was the quality of the subject matter. The subject at the Louvre was the entire evolution of "Civilization".

While there, I was even so bold to again look for an artist who had influenced me so many years previously. I like to think that it was a recollection of the religious paintings of El Greco that influenced my sky in the painting I did of a Lutheran Church in 2004. I even went so far as to consider that the contrasts of light on dark, or dark on light, from the Rembrandt works, have recurred in my outer space paintings. It was fun, to consider the possibilities. While being both humble and reverent, I was able to enjoy making observations about the techniques they'd used in their antiquated world – techniques I too had learned to manipulate in my own way. Due to his use of colours, El Greco has always been my favourite Spanish School painter. I once took a very hot and dirty ride on an old bus from Madrid to Toledo, Spain, just to view his works. I returned to his paintings in the Louvre on four separate days, and could only marvel at the way I had unconsciously used his skies; really, it seemed almost unbelievable to me.

I must raise one negative point. Unfortunately, the world of museums has changed for the worse. In fact, it may now be impossible to "study" art in many of the major museums. Tourism all over the world has swelled to such an extent that millions of people now pass by these art works every year. Even though the herds of people can be clocked at what may seem like a steady stream of five kilometres per hour (I exaggerate), the constant flashing of light bulbs, posing in front of paintings, and endless loud exclamations have changed the art museums that I knew from years ago. Digital photography, where little cost per image is involved, has done more to change the ambience of these great institutions, than anything in history.

At the Louvre, the line-up (for photographs) of the Mona Lisa is without a doubt, the most exaggerated farce in the history of art. Millions of very good reproductions exist of course, with most of them available at nominal costs, but hundreds of individuals per day, attempt to get that "one great shot". Flash bulbs bounce off of the plate glass like a constant machine gun. At first, I accidentally ended up in the queue for walking by. It seemed as if not a single person merely observed the famous masterpiece, they all just took pictures.

On my third visit to the Louvre, I was able to observe the newly renovated room for Lisa. Like the queue at a fast food restaurant this lineup was designed to move very quickly. Once in the museum, one could now get a photograph and be back onto the street in record time! Just around the corner, in a room that was only a few metres away, were paintings by members of the Italian School and seven more works by Leonardo da Vinci, every one equal to the Mona Lisa. This room also held works from the Spanish School as well as many other favourites. I wanted to shout, "Hey everybody, Veronese is just over here! Here is The Wedding Feast. You know, we call this colour "Veronese Blue", and now you can buy it in a tube!" But I didn't. I restrained myself and did my best to ignore the fiasco. Incredibly beautiful Raphael's were with the other Leonardos and I knew that literally thousands of these tourists would miss them entirely.

Instead, I enjoyed the great Raphaels for their absence of any abstraction. The Pre-Raphaelites were correct in using Raphael as their example of the contemporary turning point in art. Such was my recent study of the Masters. The positive aspect is that these paintings had brought Italian School work into the limelight. In the sixteenth century, there were over five thousand great Italian painters, without even counting their students. Again, that is one of the many mysteries of the Mona Lisa painting and its fame. I will also mention, almost as a footnote, that many of Leonardo's portraits have that same expression of mouth. After all, he was a scientist, not a painter. However, this personal discovery was all a part of my former adventure those many years ago.

Another artist whose work I noted at the Louvre was Claude Lorrain. His paintings from the 1640's were distinguished for both their sentimental and richly coloured skies; within the world of seaport scenes and as such could be considered second to none. He painted ship's riggings the way I wanted to paint riggings. Could I learn from these paintings from almost four hundred years ago? The answer was a definite and resounding – yes!

From the many paintings of the 1700's I observed a very standard method of painting suits of armour. I had begun taking notes related to my outer space paintings and I seemed to have a practical problem in painting the metal of space ships. In his 1894 painting, *Jeanne d'Arc*, Ingres had enhanced the armour's metal by adding a light brown as underpainting just below his streaking of white. This was yet another lesson from the Masters, and yet another bit of learning that had made my trip worthwhile. I would apply it to my paintings depicting the world of 2100, a future of imagined space life.

My visit the following day to the *Musée d'Orsay* made up for the preceding day's photography farce. At the temporary exhibition of the Neo-Impressionists, I was surrounded by hundreds of individuals who were truly contemplating and appreciating the views before them. I made notes as I was now seeing these works with a painter's experience. Forty years earlier, an understanding of these paintings had been above me. To understand a method – whether it is a tennis grip, a golf swing, or the manner in which a violin must be held – the method has to be brought down to a simple level. Such were my notes:

- The Neo-Impressionists used harsher colours than the Impressionists.
- Use a smaller brush on top of underpainting.
- Keep the composition simple, as best exemplified by Charles Angrand's 1889 painting, *La Seine à l'arbre*.
- Use less than four colours on each colour plateau, by trying a light green, light yellow, mid-blue and a light blue.
- Camille Pissarro used more colours, but never did he use more than four on one subject – with small brushes.
- Paint frames in a matching Pointillism for Pointillism works.
- Paint after the style of Jan Toorop, in his 1889 piece, Paysage avec Marsonnie.
- Be careful as this departure may create a style that appears Primitive. The brushes are not that small; for example, they are not like those in a Jan van Eyck work.
- To all of this remember Matisse added lines.
- Do a self-portrait in Pointillism – as a challenge.

However it was on my third day's visit to the exhibition that I finally discovered and understood the secret to painting in Pointillism. The first room of the exhibit held works that had been painted with an undercoat of yellow, after which a pale blue had been added, then finally the beach sand of the landscapes were painted in two light browns or a beige. In the second room, beige was the under-painting. The artists then used light green or light blue dots. The work in the third room used multiple under-painting colours but still then used only four or five colours in total. I had cracked the secret of Pointillism and now had learned what I had been missing. I could now finish a Neo-Impressionistic work that I had left in frustration, lying incomplete in my North Vancouver apartment.

In a previous visit I had compared the Renoirs to popular music. There are singers who are popular due to the fact that their sound can be easily imitated. There are also those who have a unique style and sound that could never be imitated. Renoir was in the latter group. In all of the temporary exhibitions I visited over the next month, I found that I was in my element. I was surrounded by small groups of knowledgeable people – literally hundreds of them. Pausing before each and every work, they shared their interests with their companions – typically, groups of two or three individuals. They communicated their pleasure, and mostly, they showed their respect for what was before them.

This was the Europe that I had remembered. The influence of this group was everywhere with the exception of the two more well known museums. It seemed that they had left these two centres to the Americans. I had especially enjoyed my return visits to the Neo-Impressionists. In these works, Cezanne was (almost) all about line. Van Gogh was about colour. Neo-Impressionism is about colour while adding the abstraction of line and therefore the contemplation of it. Line was an abstract inference. By way of their group, I could again identify with the analysis of form along with the rhythm in line.

The *Musée d'Orsay* had been an elegant railway station of the *"Belle Epoque,"* as it had been built for the 1900 Paris World's Fair. The evolution of art, continuing from the paintings exhibited at the Louvre, is perfectly displayed here as a continuum. For my purposes of both study and pure enjoyment, it is the perfect place in the world, along with its complementing Art Nouveau salons, sculpture, and exquisite architecture. I made other observations at an individual exhibition of Matisse at the Luxembourg Museum, in Luxembourg Gardens.

In his art, Matisse describes so well exactly where he was going. But he does this from the perspective of already being there. His later works therefore represent a type of Minimalism at its best. Minimalism is both an art movement and a process. In effect, the technique is the process. It follows the theory of "Found Objects" – that is, finding relevance in everyday forms, which are then re-titled and displayed within their new context. His surfaces became flat and his lines became more meaningful. They then evolved into "collages". By seeing these collages, I understood for the first time the relationship between sculpture and painting on a two dimensional surface. I was able to do this only with the help of Matisse. His works truly were the link that I needed to help me conceptualize this relationship.

Here I could readily view the evolution of artists who were each using each other's thoughts – as a unified whole – and evolving onward to Minimalism in communication, while still and simultaneously explaining everything. It had been a century of an evolution of this movement of a group of people, into expressing themselves both individually and as a unified group.

The Museum of *Zadkine*, a not-so well known Russian sculptor, was an example of something more rare in the art scene. As a cubist, his sculpture was very exceptional and his works were from the same era as Picasso and Braque. What I viewed was a house that had been converted so that its main floor now resembled what could be called a museum. The house was in an alley that seemed to be squeezed between two modern apartment buildings. No admission was charged, but I found a reason. The owners of his works made their income from selling copies of his biography and picture postcards of his work. If they had charged admission, I thought they could be accused of misrepresentation, as the number of works on display was under thirty and most of those were of carved wood. Ossip Zadkine didn't work with a conventional chisel as other sculptors did, but rather he used a hammer and saw. The resulting figures were Cubist, and evidenced the mixed styles of Leger, Dubuffet and Modigliani.

While I was visiting Paris, the Paris authorities were in process of "closing them down". The museum seemed to be open due only to the dedication of the staff. While I was there, the authorities told the staff that I was to be the last visitor until they obtained at least one of the necessary permits. Interestingly enough, they had managed to be listed in one of the more reputable guidebooks of museums in Paris. In fact, it had been from one of them that I had obtained their address. I felt glad that I'd found the place, and really enjoyed the works that I did see.

The following comprise my personal "Top Ten List" of Paris Museums that were available during my most recent visit. These are the museums that hold the art that I have always returned to visit. They house my "old friends," those works of the Masters. Years ago many of the museum names and locations were quite different, however the specific collections have remained the same, and they are now exhibited in the following venues.

1. Musée national d'Orsay – Impressionism
2. Centre Georges Pompidou – Contemporary Art
3. Musée du Louvre – Works up to 1848
4. Musée du Luxembourg – Temporary Exhibitions
5. Musée Rodin – primarily the sculpture of Rodin
6. Musée Picasso – Included are other works
7. Musée du Marmottan – The works of Monet
8. Musée du Grand Palais – Temporary Exhibitions
9. Musée de Carnavalet – Temporary Exhibitions
10. Musée de la Musique (Cité) – 900 instruments

All of the "top ten" museums have temporary but meticulously planned exhibitions within their premises. It is not possible to list these, as each exhibition offers a varying collection of painting and sculpture. Of course, personal interests of the viewer will always dictate their enthusiasm for undertaking the adventure each museum presents. I found that all of these museums required at least two or three days of repeated visits.

I also did not list addresses or specifics; I leave that to the travel writers. The museums change constantly as renovations are ongoing. My second temptation was to translate the names to English, however this is the Parisian list of permanent art work. To change it would be to change the experience. I have also not made reference to the fabulous experience of architecture in Paris. All of these museums are incredible buildings, either as historic or contemporary references of beauty.

My personal experience has included the same type of national displays in what is now a list of forty-five countries, and that list keeps growing. These travels have been planned as destinations in the world of great art. To imagine, as an example, having contemplated Van Gogh without including the experience of the Van Gogh Museum, in Amsterdam, would be impossible. The same is true of the German contemporary painters, whom I most enjoy finding and contemplating when they are displayed at their best, in their home German cities.

My writing here also has not made any attempt to concentrate on periods other than my focus on the present one hundred years of modern change. There are well over fifty main museums in Paris. Each is of great interest to many individuals, as we go through life with our many and differing tastes. Paris is only one art destination, but it's a great one!

In the 1840's Balzac wrote: "*In Paris there are certain streets which have fallen into as much disrepute as a man branded with infamy; there are also noble streets, straightforwardly decent streets and young streets upon whose morality the public has not yet formed an opinion; there are murderous streets, streets more ancient than the most aged dowagers, respectable streets, streets which are always clean, streets which are always dirty, working-class, industrious, mercantile streets. In short, the streets of Paris have human qualities, and their physiognomy imprints certain ideas in us against which we are totally defenceless...*

These observations, which would be incomprehensible outside Paris, will doubtless be seized upon by those men of learning and reflection, of poetry and pleasure, who, wandering within the city walls, feast on the delectable enjoyments it offers from morning till night; by those who find Paris the most delightful of monsters: a pretty woman at times, at others a miserable old hag; as freshly minted as a new coin here, as elegant as a lady of fashion there."

Paris is still the same monstrous miracle, an extraordinary assembly of movement, machines and thoughts, the city of a thousand novels, the brains behind the world. Such was the Paris of almost two centuries ago to the well-known writer known to most people as simply Balzac. After living in Paris a number of cold winter months, I can say that completely independent of this, and without any knowledge of a similar metaphor,

I wrote the following prior to reading Balzac, in 1966: "*Paris is like a sophisticated and grand old whore – beautiful from a distance, but wretchedly ugly when viewed closely in detail.*" The only other thing that I can say in comparing myself to the life of Balzac is that the girl

I wrote this to, who happened to live in then very conservative Western Canada - immediately dumped me and stated a reference to my *creative* writing. Where this was consistent with the life and thoughts of the famous Balzac, at the time I felt I had an allied (although dead) compatriot.

Thus I present my insistence that we be ourselves in art. Without individual communication of that which we believe, or that which we seemed compelled to focus upon, there is no art. It could be only a handicraft. One thing was certain as I toured the new Paris of this twenty-first century. The city was no longer spotted with art galleries flaunting their newly found creations. The Paris art galleries that I had known were from the past and galleries were now almost non-existent. The art that I did see in galleries was tired. It was from the past and seemed to be the same as when I had left the city forty years earlier.

A booklet called *Envue* listed the temporary art exhibits that were now being held in libraries of each of the quarters of the city. When the government is the only supporter or patron of the arts, it is a sure sign that the arts are not flourishing. To think that art was thriving in Paris in the twenty-first century would be very naïve. It seemed that nothing in art in Paris, France, was exciting now.

As a secondary stop for the day, I visited an advertised arts and crafts market at the foot of the Montparnasse tower. Upon arriving and observing, my first emotion was excitement, and the immediate thought that, "They had moved." Just as it had been forty years before among the artists who exhibited at Place du Tertre, there seemed to be a handful of painters who were actually creating art – and I seemed to have found the place where they had located themselves. A number of the sculptors were very good, as were two or three of the contemporary painters. They were selling their works for the same price as the tourist souvenir "terrible stuff" at *Place du Tertre*. I like to believe in art being attainable directly from the artist, and available at a price that's not impossible for a salaried consumer. I'm not a socialist, but it just seems sensible. Direct selling of unique works does exist, as it should – even in Paris. I was happy to hang out there for a few hours. The market was called the "*Marché de la Creation*" and it had a nice feel to it. Here were approximately one hundred and twenty artists, each with their own stall. By each having an organized display space, the presentation was superior to Place du Tertre. The greatest strength of the presentations was the incredible contemporary sculpture as a mix.

In visiting the Fine Arts Museum in Chartres, I was reminded of the *Place du Tertre's* level of painting during the 1960's. Both Soutine and Vlaminck were being displayed there. I knew that Vlaminck as well as Maurice Utrillo had been Place du Tertre street painters who had "made good." They were both colourists and for that reason I identified with them considerably. The landscapes of Vlaminck were very specific. His technique, colour and use of the palette knife had dictated a familiar style which had been replicated often, as was commonly done in other Place du Tertre street paintings by the many painters there. The use of colour and texture could not have been more identical unless the goal had been to copy, which it wasn't. The goal was simply to provide emotional beauty – as in using blues similar to those in a Vlaminck painting.

Thousands of these paintings now hang all around the world. In many cases the owners of these street scenes are not aware of what the artist was communicating or even trying to replicate. They are simply enjoying them, which is great.

On yet another weekend, I discovered a second, "*Marché Parisien de la Création*". It was larger and it seemed more successful than the other. The paintings here seemed superior to any other of the Paris presentations. These painters could have been presented in the local art galleries, or quite possibly, they would be presented in the finest galleries in the future. This market was just off Place Bastille on Boulevard Richard Lenoir. Both markets advertised themselves as presenting contemporary art, and they both did that well.

The first took place each Sunday, all year round, and the second was each Saturday, all year as well. In all art marketing, there has to be an entry level. There also has to be that balance where the art consumer can find, and be the patron of, the rising star. These two locations provided that possibility. I felt exceptionally pleased that it still existed.

No two human beings are similarly gifted in sensory capacity, in intelligence, in the ability to conceptualize abstraction, or in a talent for appreciation of fantasy. The ability to appreciate art may be linked to the ability to think abstractly, which in turn is said to be precisely what education develops. Appreciation of music, drama, dance, or painting is inconsistent. A passionate music lover may have not developed a visual taste. Drama lovers can be totally illiterate about music and vice versa. Despite historical assumptions, there has never been a single, all purpose cultural elite group who define the sense of a general arts appreciation.

Secondly, the existence of a broad, amateur-based movement in the arts reinforces professionalism by building the cultural public, not only quantitatively, but also qualitatively. It makes it possible for the individual to gain skill and taste, at their personal choice of speed, as he or she ascends towards connoisseurship. It keeps a public interested in the arts, while creating education by initiating discussions. It is consistently building art appreciation, while heightening aesthetic sensitivity.

Thirdly, the creation process within any of the arts involves not merely financial analysis of cash flow, but encourages a series of complex social arrangements and motivations that make it possible. For this reason, the benefits of art cannot be restricted to an affluent few. Art is always in need of culture consumers; however, both the financial and mental variances of all of the existing consumer levels need to be satisfied. According to this premise, even Place du Tertre "tourist works" might conceivably be justified. However, the main reason that they cannot be justified as art is that they do not live up to the definition of art as "an evocation of a state of mind;" thus, they are left defined as handicraft at best.

Only half a century ago art galleries could be spotted around Paris in incredibly large numbers. I'd discovered that only a few art galleries now remained on the Left Bank and Montmartre; these were shamefully tourist level in their presentations. Still, I believed that there must still be a place where, within a couple of blocks in area, two-dozen or so art galleries could survive.

Thankfully, such a place does exist, on *Rue de Pas de la Mule* and the abutting *Place des Vosges*. At Place des Vosges I finally discovered the commercial art galleries that I'd presumed I would find somewhere. Conveniently, it is only two blocks from the "*Marché Parisien de la Création*" at Bastille. I somehow felt justified as a painter that consumerism in art was alive and well in one of the corners of Paris. I was possibly one of the last to discover this, even as the English speaking market swarmed with the business of those thousands of hungry-for-art buyers.

From my observations of popular styles within the paintings that seemed to be selling, I made more notes:

- Do a collage with music notations showing.
- Use a brown stain varnish on a few landscape works.
- Paint a few inferred nude figures using lines.
- Use more Matisse-style highlighted drawing.
- Paint a few non-objective works on wrinkled, crumpled-up canvas.
- Use gold highlighting on vivid-colour abstraction.

• Use silver metal rods in Constructivism mode, creating wall sculpture.

• Do Linear Cubism study of country fields (green trees, orange and yellow fields, five colours or less), with much texture.

• The three most important popular items in Parisian painting seem to be, texture, texture and texture.

In accompaniment to this were the same artists and their colleagues from around France, displaying and selling through what was billed as the "*Grand Marché d'Art Contemporain.*" In English this translates as the "large market of contemporary art." These were presentations by the artists within tent kiosks set up in rows. There were as many as 480 artists in each market, but these markets only existed for five consecutive days, twice per year. These were what had finally taken any of the remaining better artists away from Place du Tertre, in Montmartre. They also seemed to be well used by young art school graduates.

In perusing the old addresses of the Left Bank in detail, I finally found one corner where I could see signs of two-dozen art galleries. It was the intersection of the three streets of rue *Mazarine*, rue *Jacques Callo*t and rue *Guénégaud*. The rest of the detail is that none of these commercial galleries were open more than three days per week, and even then, only for limited hours. Some were only arranging private showings, the rigid marketing concept of "by appointment." Even though they were selling exquisite works, their intention was only to display to qualified buyers. The level of patience required of anyone needing to return at an appointed hour was certainly going to exclude all but the most interested consumer.

In the brief time I spent walking about, I observed many international buyers trying doors, voicing their dissatisfaction at the process, and walking away expressing their disbelief at not being able to buy anything instantly. The first point these consumers of art may not have recognized is that the galleries were no longer economically viable. If they had been staffed as in any normal retail outlet outside of Paris, it would have created a negative cash flow.

Secondly, and on the positive side, was a deeply ingrained notion that had been brought forward from the past two centuries of French Salon Painting. Given the traditional European-based perception that elitism is that which most individuals seek or strive towards, the French gallery owners seemed to presume that they were providing something of a service. This was an overview that the potential consumers from North American had simply not understood. Most non-French would feel awkward ringing the bell to arrange an appointment. It was assumed by the gallery owner, that once inside, the client could be more relaxed in a private showing.

Along with this follows the presumption that their relationship with the work could be different and more intimate than in a more public process. What was being offered was the opportunity of feeling more special, and being treated more personally, while enjoying the works of art. However, this merely illustrates one of the cultural differences between North American and European thought. Unfortunately, it is the French artists who suffer for their lack of contemporary marketing methodology.

I learned that the *Beaux Arts* University Expositions of student paintings, traditionally held in their large library auditorium, were now held only once each year. The focus was on works oriented more to the architectural field. Other art colleges had replaced the antiquated Beaux Arts and there were now seven hundred and fifty art schools listed in France. They offered programs in Applied Art, Graphic Arts, Beaux-Arts, and Multimedia. No longer was the prestige of the ancient university an advantage when weighed against the contemporary end production of each student of painting.

I reminded myself of how fortunate I had been to have actually experienced the ambience, and to have felt myself a part of the old Paris – that Paris of the painters and writers of the first part of the twentieth century!

With this had come the traditions of Parisian life, with its varying styles of ambience delegated to each individual part, or quarter, of town. It was also easy to realize that without a doubt I had been part of the last generation to ever "dress up" in order to walk comfortably down the once beautiful Champs Elysées. Just as the artist's ease within a once-great city which welcomed creativity had disappeared, the uniqueness of the area surrounding the Champs Elysées had been unmistakably diminished.

This glorious main street known all over the world as being from a time of the wonderful French architecture of the "*belle époque*" had become an almost seedy environment. The once elite storefronts had become a series of stores that were selling sunglasses or inexpensive clothes, along with the ever-present fast food restaurants. Many young couples now arrive hourly in hopes of viewing the former world of the Champs Elysées. Cheap trinkets and other paraphernalia are offered in a kiosk selling style, in lieu of a world that existed only half of a century ago. Understanding and coming to personal terms with the death of the Paris of the Arts, was very similar to the grieving process relative to the death of an old friend. As someone dies, someone else is born. The arts are very much alive and well now in other cities, and throughout other countries.

What I had formerly experienced was the last phase in the life of old Paris. Like revering an old friend, I was humbled that I had known that period of its life. I had now lived in Paris again, revisited my favourite museums, contemplated life's changing themes, and had arrived at a few seasoned conclusions.

I finally found myself taking a break only a few feet from the oldest zoo in the world. It hadn't changed – however, ironically, perhaps the zoo was one thing that really needed change. In those same gardens stood the antiquated Museum of Palaeontology. Once, I had even made more notes to myself there as I had a plan to paint some outer space paintings that would include dinosaurs. I'd noted that I'd need to pay attention to the detail that their accented teeth were part of their skeleton. This wasn't any major earth-shaking note; it was just a painter's observation of detail.

This area where I was sitting was called the *Jardin des Plantes*, and I just sat enjoying the natural ambience of this end of the day. As I observed my colleagues, I realized that many of the grey-haired individuals sitting around me, may well have been the same people I had sat near at the area's sidewalk cafés so many years ago.

Life is about choice. I knew I could sit here or at other similar spots, and watch and enjoy the beautiful flowers, gorgeous shrubberies, and the beauty of the setting sun – or that I could get up and go onward to enjoying more of the adventure in art that this world has to offer. I chose the latter.

As if to amplify my feelings, my visit to the Pavillon de L'Arsenal the following day concluded with the perfect setting. Here the city of Paris was presenting its past, present and future, as it related to Urban Planning. The Pavilion had become a centre of information and the *"Exposition of Urbanization and Architecture of Paris."* Models of the old city were there, as were the present statistics. The future of Paris was presented both in model form and with computerized projections. I doubt that Paris will ever be the futuristic centre that the models seem to present as historic Paris will always be evident. However, the combination of its past with this unique space age architecture, will once again give it an individual flair.

For that, as a city, it will once again become unique to the world. On the way to the presentation, I happened to pass a foreign couple who were rather loudly proclaiming their frustration at not being able to quietly walk together, in a romantic setting, along the banks of the Seine. What seemed like thousands of people had crowded about them, visitors trying to capture the magic of a Paris that has passed into antiquity.

We all had pursued that – whether it was the writer's Paris that endured up to the fifties, or the turn of the last century "*à la Belle Époque.*" The strolling couple would have been astounded by the projections for the future of only 2035. The models showed a tremendous building growing up the banks of the Seine – a large commercial community. Later, I did meet others who were more than content to just stroll in the existing Paris. Their more positive remarks, as they really enjoyed the beauty of the day, reminded me that the nature of Paris is in "the eye of the beholder." This architectural presentation had been not just about the fact that mega high rise projects were about to be built; it was about the facts relative to the use of the banks of the Seine.

The "quiet" riverbanks were about to become beautifully designed contemporary structures. Concrete, glass, and the shining metal look of the next century were consistent with these approved construction projects. Being Paris, ever changing art was very much a part of this town plan concept. As if to amplify my own feelings, I thought of the Paris street scenes of almost half a century ago. I concluded that I would focus on my outer space paintings – and the very optimistic future of art.

In saying my goodbye to Paris, I made a symbolic trip to the Luxembourg Gardens, on the Left Bank. It was here that I had spent much time with my international circle of friends - so long ago. I had left these gardens to begin a family and to pursue a career that would support a certain lifestyle. I had now completed that cycle and could now leave Luxembourg Gardens to become the painter and writer that I had wanted to become in the first place.

This second cycle was more about creative freedom. It was potentially about the next one-third of my life. Paris could again be left behind and simultaneously stay a small part of me. Whether created in the tropics, in our northern terrain, or by imagination within the outer universe, I knew my art would always have some reflection of that which initially trained and impressed me in Paris, so many years ago. I had now reflected on my training ground, and even relived a bit of it – and with that I had found contentment.

PART 3 OPEN SEA

Plate 1 Lone Arbutus Tree At Storm's Break
14" x 18", acrylic on canvas board

A Gulf Island windward view, this composition is extremely free. The lines of the landscape swing in broad sweeps across the picture, and are framed on the left by the tall curving tree. This leads the eye into the break of the storm itself, allowing one to experience the contradictory nature of the two simultaneous weather systems. By adopting a high viewpoint in relation to the objects, the shapes take on a character sympathetic to the plane of the picture surface. We see that structure is given to a painting by the considered relationship of its constituent colours – and that composition in itself serves as an element at the painter's disposal for the expression of his feelings. This was to be evocation of duration and a moment of order and therefore clarity of form and expression as purity of sensation.

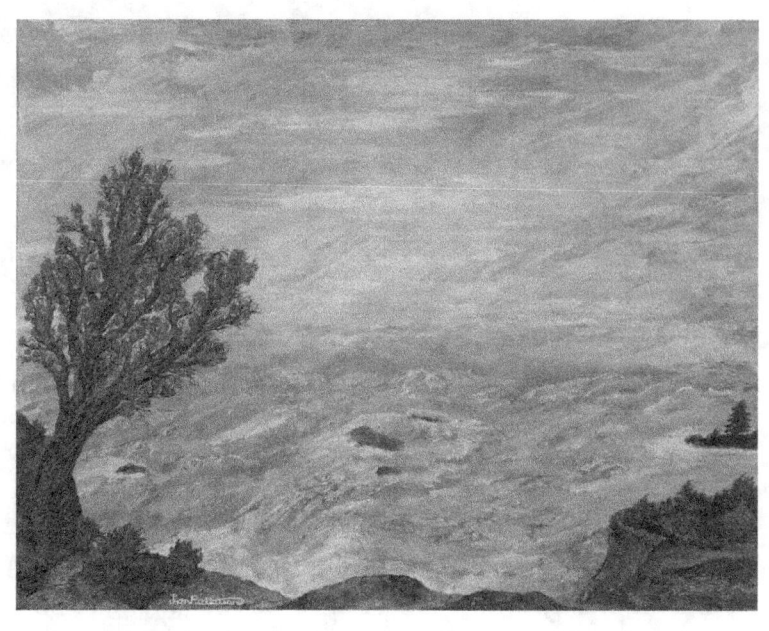

Plate 2 Oceanic Sunset 14" X 18", acrylic on canvas

Here all is poetic invention, a transformation of the actual. The goal was to capture the play of the golden light of sunset at a moment when the sun, still almost invisible, dominates the clear sea air, flooding the sky with a light that seems unreal. The composition centres on the heavenly body that will soon fall below the horizon as the waves direct the eye to retain that focus. This aspiration to measureless distance adds the gravity of poetry to the enchantment and is in itself an achievement. The painterly style called Mannerism originally described a period of art in Italy during the second half of the 16th century, when the rationality of the Renaissance was beginning to be distorted and strained. Its overemphasis on a distinctive mode of expression dominates and tends to eclipse the feeling expressed. Personal mannerisms relative to the style of the artist are no longer considered detrimental, but are deemed essential in evoking a particular state of mind. Mannerism is evident not only in this work but also in many of my other paintings of ships. The works are painted with sentiment revealed by slight distortions or exaggerations of the subject matter. The application of the style may be seen in both Oceanic Sunset and the following.

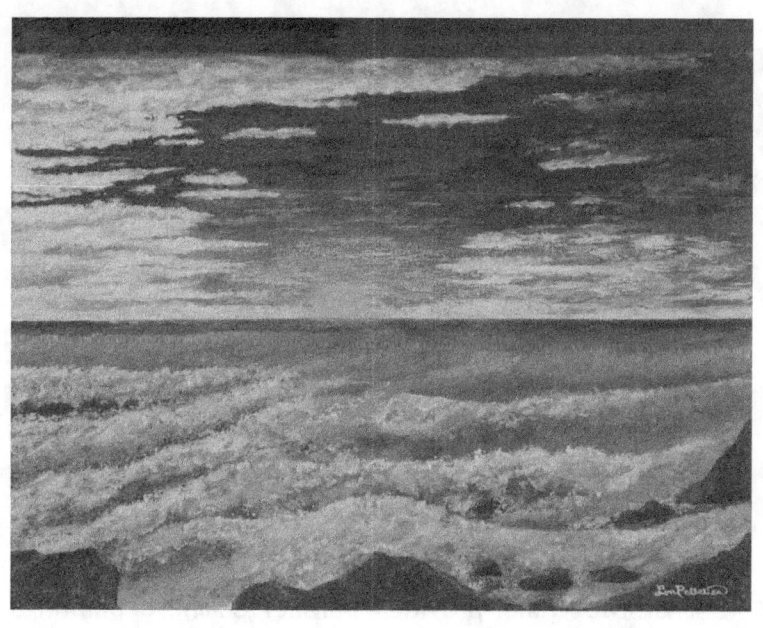

Plate 3 Killer Whale Festival 16" X 20", acrylic on canvas board

When the tendency to idealize becomes so important a mannerism that the work completely embellishes form, all that remains is satire. The subject here is an obvious reference to those tourist-focused paintings that have evolved to meet consumer demand – in this case, a pod of playful whales. The work becomes nonsensical and illustrates the epitome of jumping whales designed to hang "above the fireplace." Initially painted with the sole intention of satire, compositional elements were then used to enhance this work. For the Pacific Coast artist, the whales provide a parallel to Alberta paintings of "horses in moonlight." By using satire, the painting can rise to become art, in lieu of producing those paintings most dreaded by trained artists, those of "calendar art" or strictly "commercial painting.

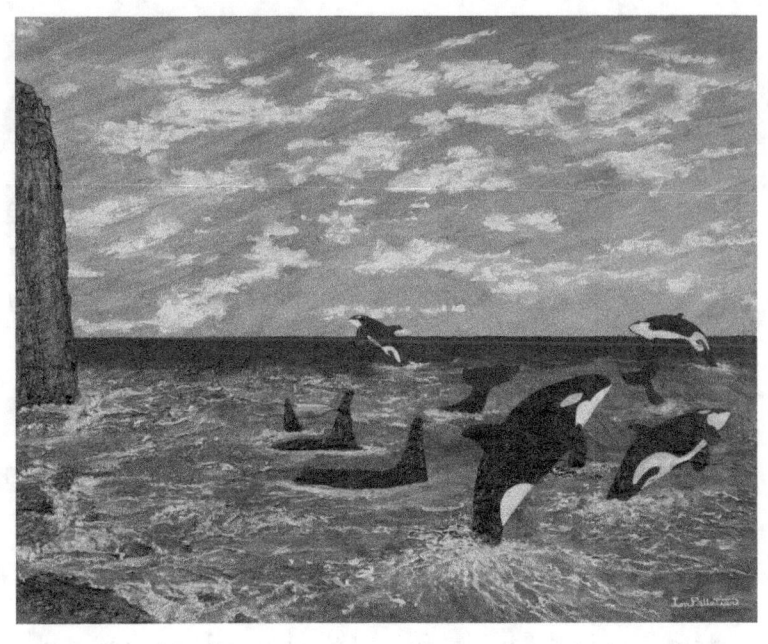

Plate 4 The Endeavour 16" X 20", acrylic on canvas

This night view of Captain Cook's Endeavour anchored in 1770 shows her as a typical British East Indiaman barque. She was 97.5 feet stem to stern, had a beam of 12.25 feet and a 19-foot draft. She was used on his first voyage of discovery, from 1768 to 1771. His later ship was The Resolution. In painting this, I advanced through the entire canvas at the same time, creating a kind of conversation among the colours, tones and lines already in progress; these were then used throughout the rest of the painting. Not entirely absorbed in draftsmanship, but in the active interplay between the blue with whites, I tried to portray the way the ship seems to quiver in the brightness of the contrasting moonlight. In this manner the work may surpass mere illustration.

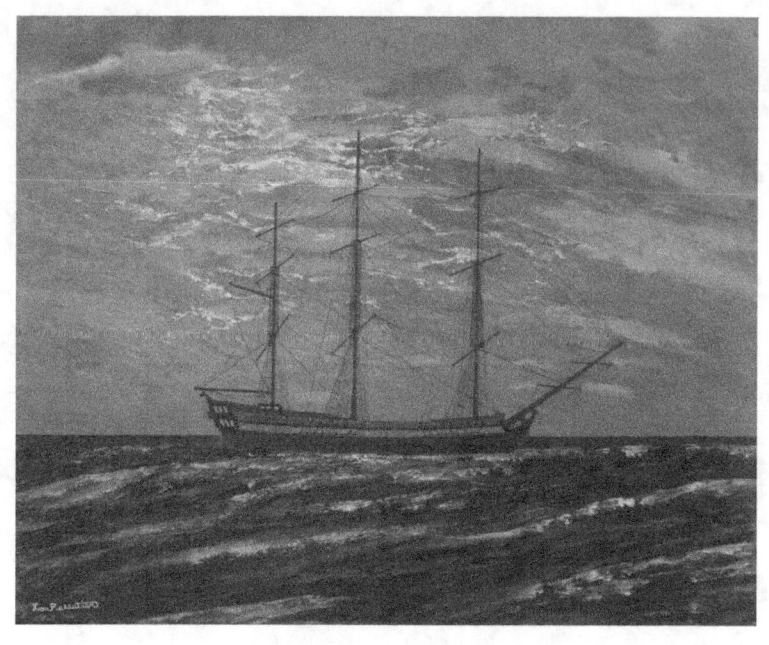

Plate 5 Baltimore Schooner 16" X 20", acrylic on canvas

This was the beauty of sailing in the 1800's. The vigorous and crackling brilliance of the brush strokes show gradations in the depth of the water by their applied pigment. Just as they do in nature, the sweep of the clouds and the rake of the masts complement each other. The lines become evocative of movement. Detail and colour become secondary to the story of the painting.

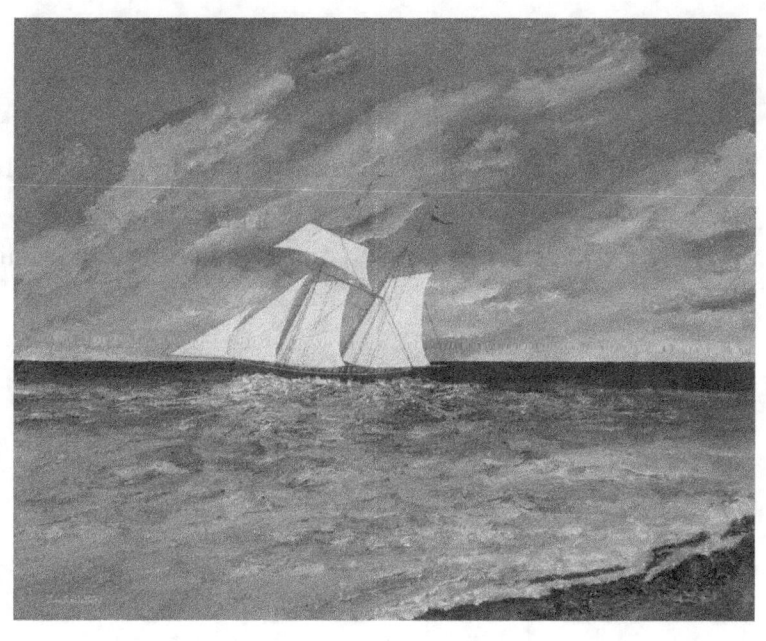

Plate 6 Safe Harbour 14" X 18", acrylic on canvas

Like the more Impressionistic works, this exemplifies the search for a construction after nature. The expression is of serenity at the calmness of the bay as a shelter, and was painted within the ambience of the Gulf Islands.

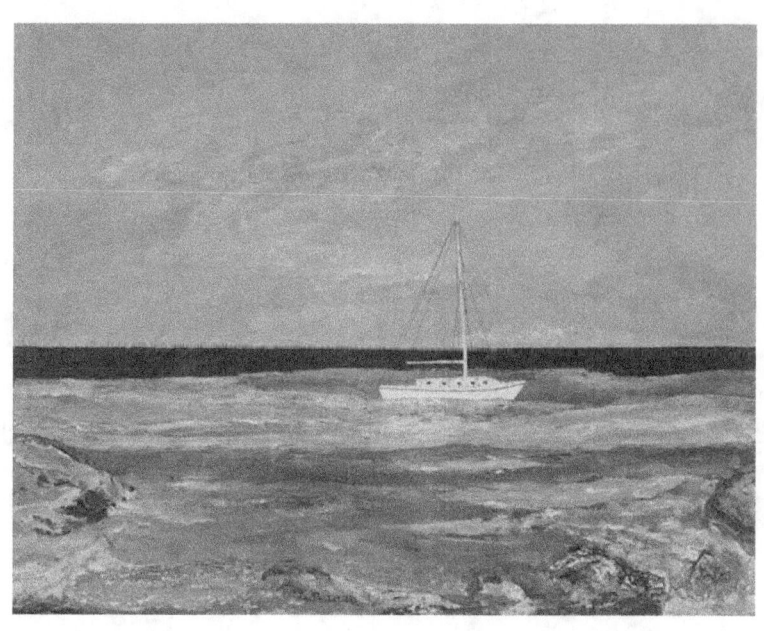

Plate 7 Rough Sea 11" X 15", acrylic on canvas

With its controlled use of colour, this presents an adoption of a more painterly style and also of Expressionism. The work provided an excuse to use an exquisite colour harmony. While it offers a somewhat distorted vision of Naturalism, the elements of restlessly energetic self-expression exist, and depict a spectrally heightened and distorted reality. It has an arabesque rhythm and a reliance on both subjective inspiration and introspection.

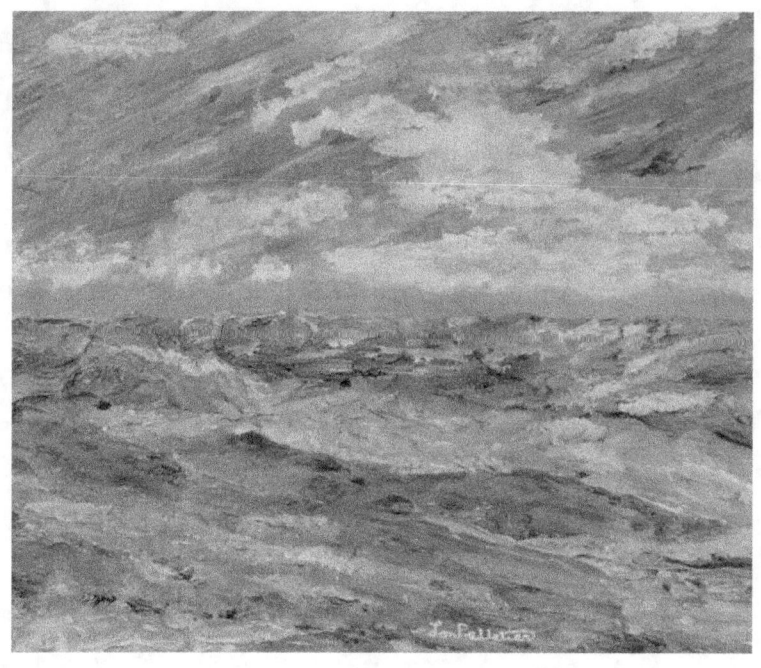

Plate 8 Ocean Breeze 14" X 18",
acrylic on canvas board

When compared to elements of my other paintings with similar themes, this work is more sensitive. In it I have applied myself to the perfection of the rendering, with a complete focus on my feelings for the sea and the force of its nature.

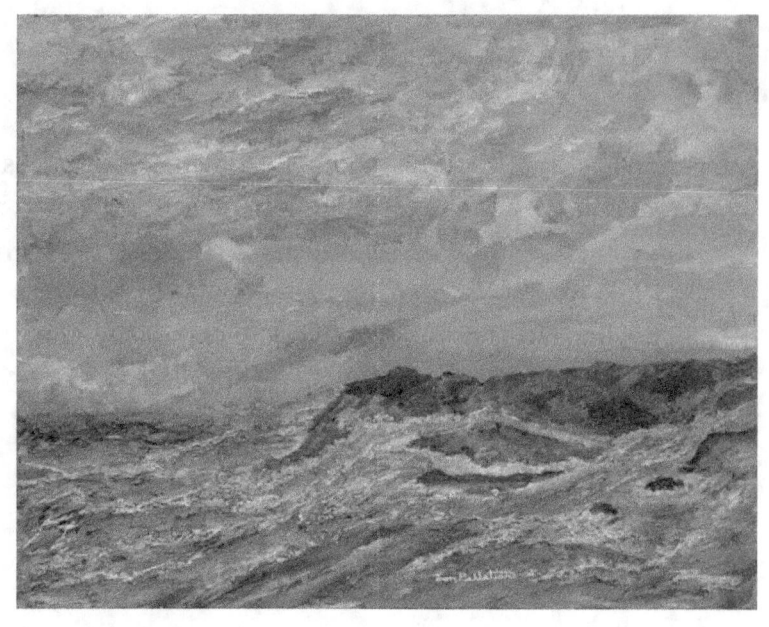

Plate 9 Whale Pod Horizon 14" X 18",
acrylic on canvas board

The composition is overstated to show the waves
working on the shoreline. The canvas is alive with
interacting rhythms with references to surface and depth
and there has been purposeful attention to both the
opaque and the transparent. In reality, this is the more
normal whale pod viewing and in that, there is satisfaction
both for the observer and for the artist.

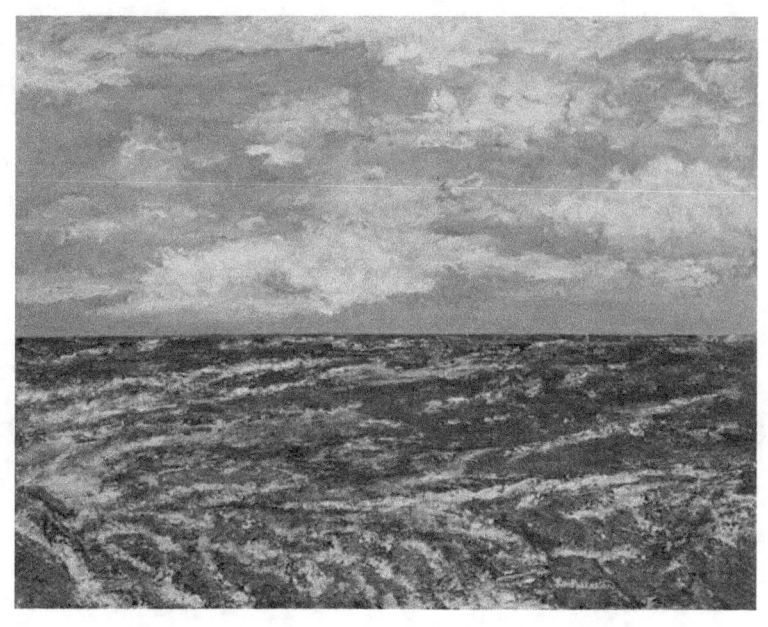

Plate 10 The Flying Cloud 22" X 30",
acrylic on canvas

Fully rigged on the foremast, mainmast and mizzen mast - with topmast staysail - and fore royal studding sail - and fore topgallant studding sails flying. In 1850 she covered the run from New York to San Francisco in 89 days, a record that was never surpassed. Utilizing perspective, composition and literary allusions from classical sources, this work has become a favourite among those who admire tall ship paintings. Within the details of the tall ship paintings, the following terms are related and as details can be often viewed.

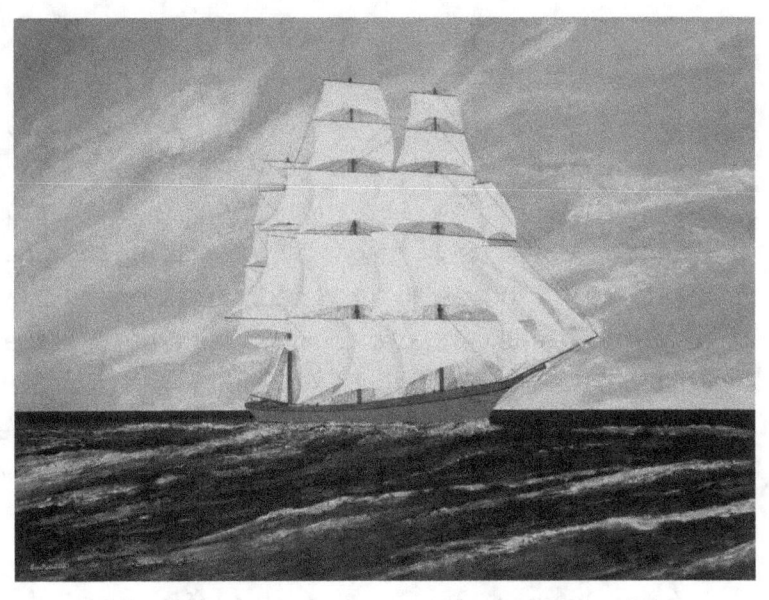

Plate 11 - 1641 Sailing To New France 14" X 18", acrylic on canvas board

The subject is an approximation of the ship that transported Guillaume, Michelle and Jean Pelletier from France to what is now Canada. The wave action showing a constant force forward in the water to the right, evocative of a cry of "steady as she goes", along with the tilt of the boat into the onward goal - is important to the work. 59 Part 3 - Open Sea We become conscious of qualities other than those of mere representation with a different type of pictorial substance. The space is carved out clearly with the ship taking its place in accordance with the planes defining the space, and with the values of its hues.

As taken from the text of the novel, "Pelletier Chronicles - 500 Years": "Their ship was of a design called a Caravel. She was a fifteenth-and sixteenth century cargo vessel, that displaced about two hundred tons - rigged with three masts and a bowsprit at the most forward part of the boat, lateen sails with frequently used square sails on the fore masts, along with a sprit sail. She was gaff-rigged with a four-sided mainsail whose top edge is supported by a spar call a gaff. A halyard hoisted and controlled each sail."

The technique of scale drawing appeared from the seventeenth-century onward; therefore, with these ships for the first time the frame was built first. They were rigged with up to three masts, with a mizzen-mast, the mast nearest the stern, stepped on the transom. This allowed sailing close to the wind for efficiency. "Unless the ship's awkward motion prevented it, the sailors had been busy reaming up the standing rigging, holystoning the deck boards and scrubbing the main bower cable. It was a distinct air of brisk, well-disciplined determination."

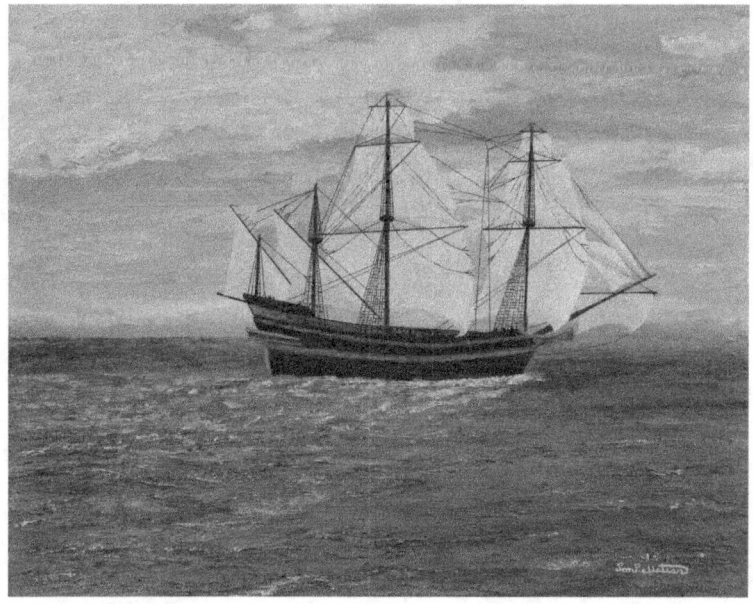

Plate 12 Clipper Ship I - The Christian Radich
18" X 24", acrylic on canvas board

The work was painted from photographs in 2003. The ship was built in 1937 in Norway, and she is a frequent participant in Tall Ship races and films. The mood of this painting is one of reverie.

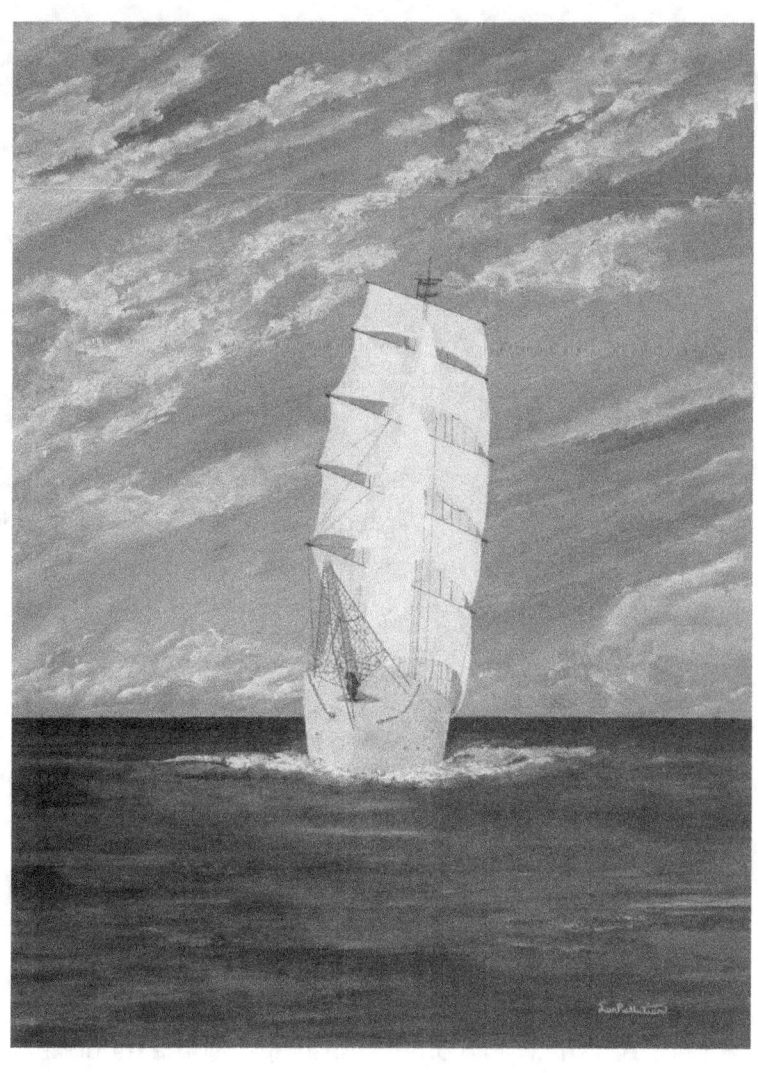

Plate 13 Clipper Ship II 16" X 20", acrylic on canvas

Painted in 2002 from a group of sail plans of the 1850's. This ship is quite similar to the Flying Cloud, however the sails here are rigged differently. The waves show her to be initiating a coming about for a starboard tack. Here are geometric elements of the tall ship coupled with the beauty of light.

As taken from the text of the novel, "Pelletier Chronicles - 500 Years": "They moved slowly and deliberately up the ratlines. At length, about three would shuffle out along each yardarm, both port and starboard, feeling for the foot ropes as they went. The bark was then swaying fifty to seventy feet below. These masts yawed and arched across the sky as their hands clawed at the heavy wet canvass with freezing fingers struggling to tie off the reefing pennants while the wind whipped at the lines. A bight of loosened canvas, caught by a gust, could render a man insensible or knock him clean off of the yardarm. "Frequently too much speed was gained as she surfed down the biggest waves' backs. This sinking feeling was dependant on the helmsmen as he simultaneously kept a true course. Lifting high on a swell roaring under her stern she would often smash against the rudder blade as the helmsman struggled against the wheel's kick."

"The outcome upon occasion was tattered sails streaming in the wind. Lines and reefing pennants thrashed and snaked wildly, smashing blocks and clattering against the masts. Broken yards hung askew and upper ratlines drooped slack and lifeless. Shrouds were frayed to thread with much of the rigging gone. Work was then simply scheduled to refurbish all that was broken. Land had to be reached in some manner."

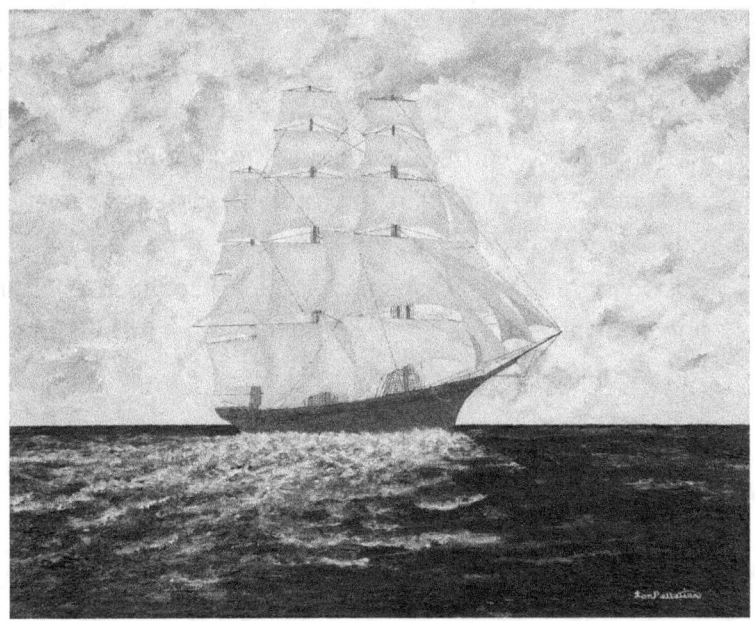

Plate 14 Clipper Ship III - The Ariel 20" X 24", acrylic on canvas board

The work was painted from archived charcoal sketches in 2003. The Ariel was one of the fastest Tea Clippers of 1865. She was 197 feet with a beam of almost 34 feet at 853 tons. She once made the voyage from China to the USA in 99 days. The composition is built on two large arcs as arrows thrusting forward; with a rise forming on the creation of the waves. This arc is repeated in the upper curve of the clouds and as such, significance lies in line and pattern. The lines model insofar as they express the essentials of form.

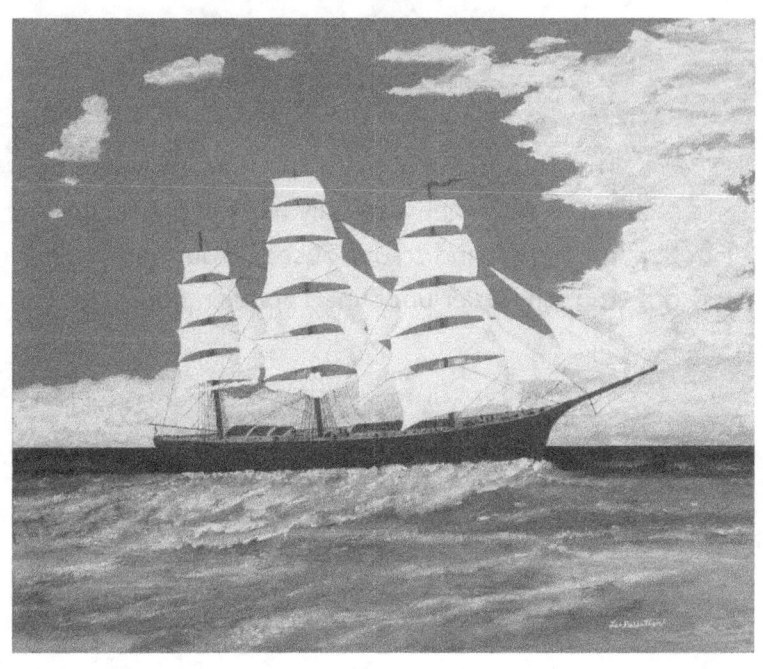

Plate 15 Ocean Surf 14" X 18",
acrylic on canvas board

The positioning of the boat, although seeming
haphazard, is extremely carefully worked out relative to
both composition and colour. Fused colour harmonies and
strong, though rather undefined poetic mood.

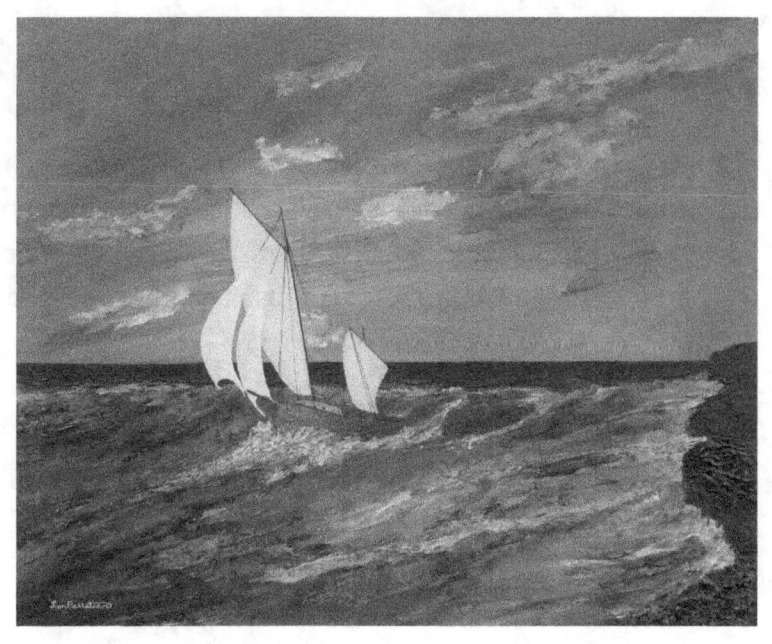

Plate 16 Sailing Silhouette 14" X 18", acrylic on canvas

The white silhouette of the sailboat is enhanced by the general colour scheme, which is of an overall blue and white, corresponding with a faint grayness in all the tones. It is almost monochromatic, with just a bit of glamorized light on the silhouetted sailboat.

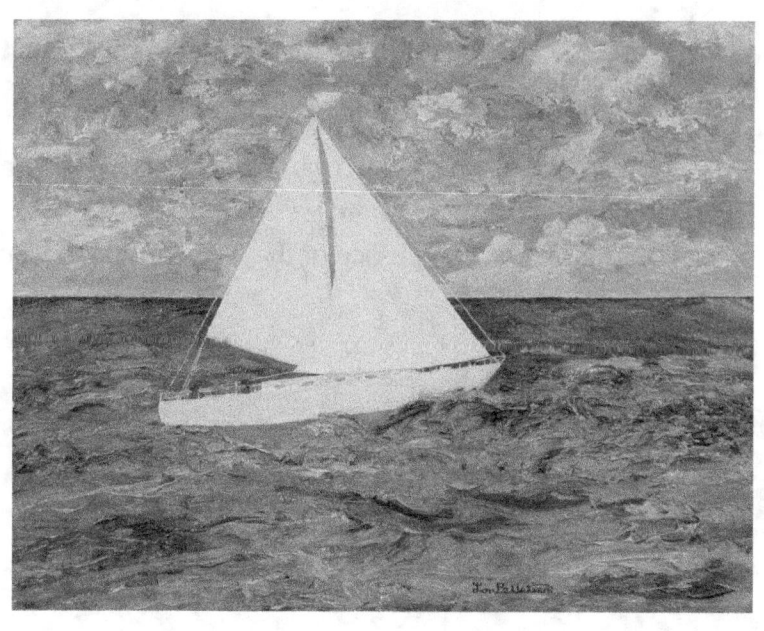

Plate 17 Wind In The Sails 16" X 20",
acrylic on canvas board

Simple interpretation of the feeling of the sea was
the intention. The response to nature is direct, as the
painter relives the experience of the ocean, the mist, and
the rolling waves.

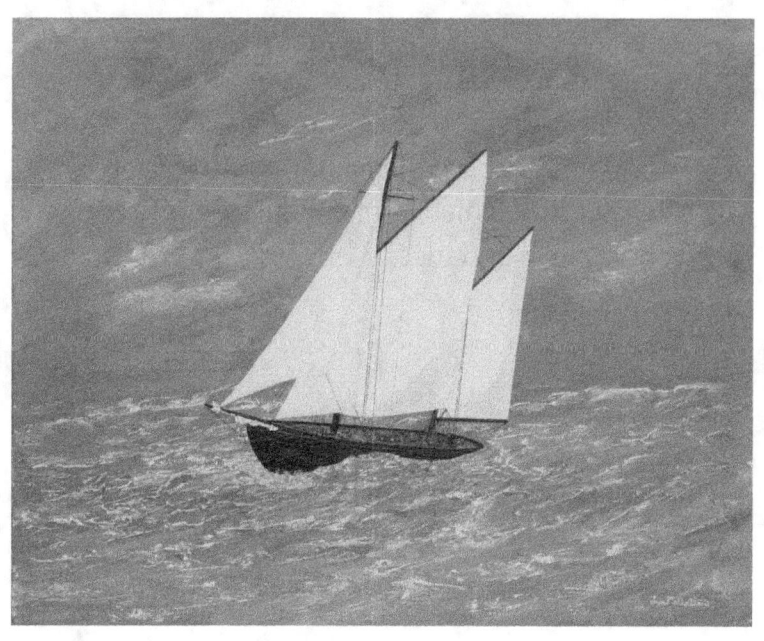

Plate 18 Early Morning Blow 12" X 16",
acrylic on canvas board

Very strict and elemental in its feeling, this is a
painting of the elements, where the sailboat becomes
secondary in importance.

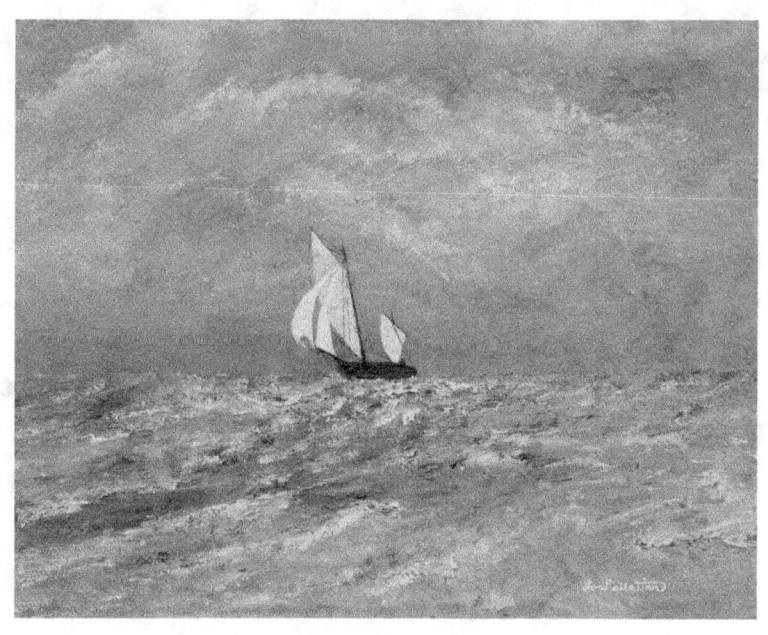

Plate 19 Zuider Zee Sailing 14" X 18",
acrylic on canvas

There are traditional eighteenth century sailboats, as well as the older houses of Marken on the shore. These were painted after viewing the subject, from various sketches made in Holland in 2000.

A technique of making the vigorous brush strokes obvious, is used throughout the piece. Unfortunately the combination of its picturesque charm tends to create a kind of "calendar art".

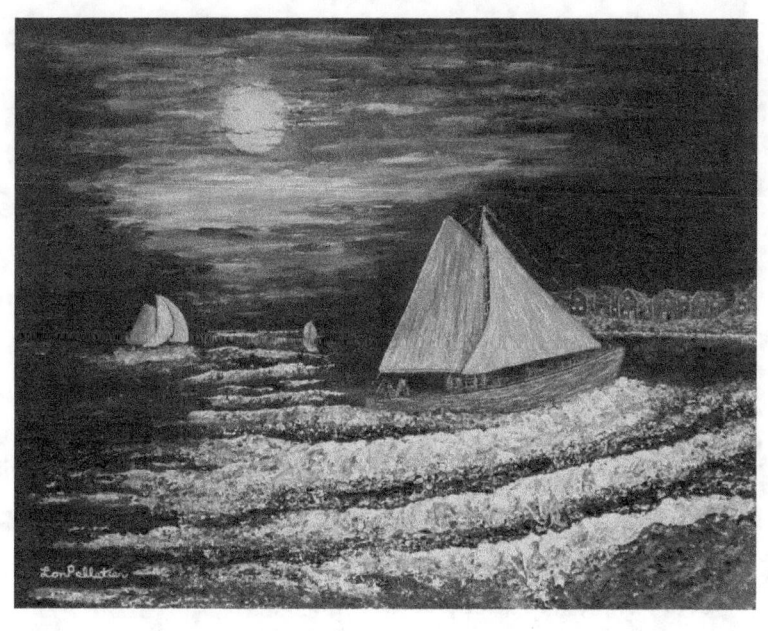

Plate 20 Pointillism At Sail 20" X 24",
acrylic on canvas

Neo-Impressionism, a more systemized development of Impressionism, follows the physical laws of light and colour combinations. It uses a precise technique with organized dots of pure, related colour. This is also sometimes called Divisionism or Pointillism depending on technique. By using it, optical mixtures of more brilliant colours are obtained.

The Neo-Impressionists were more concerned with the forms and compositional structures of their paintings than were the more spontaneous Impressionists. Everything is reduced to the mere sensation given by the eye's retina. Painting these small dots of colour, which the observer's eyes must mix, is an exciting process for the painter. As each individual dot is set upon the canvas, the colours change their normal purity.

Just as Jazz is often called a musician's music, Pointillism is a painter's painting. Although it is tedious to paint, it is also a lot of fun, as the paints seem to change their individual colour immediately upon application. When viewing the end result, the eye sees only a summary of the overall colour, a message that is then communicated to the brain. Traditionally, the Masters painted their frames with the same technique, as was also done here.

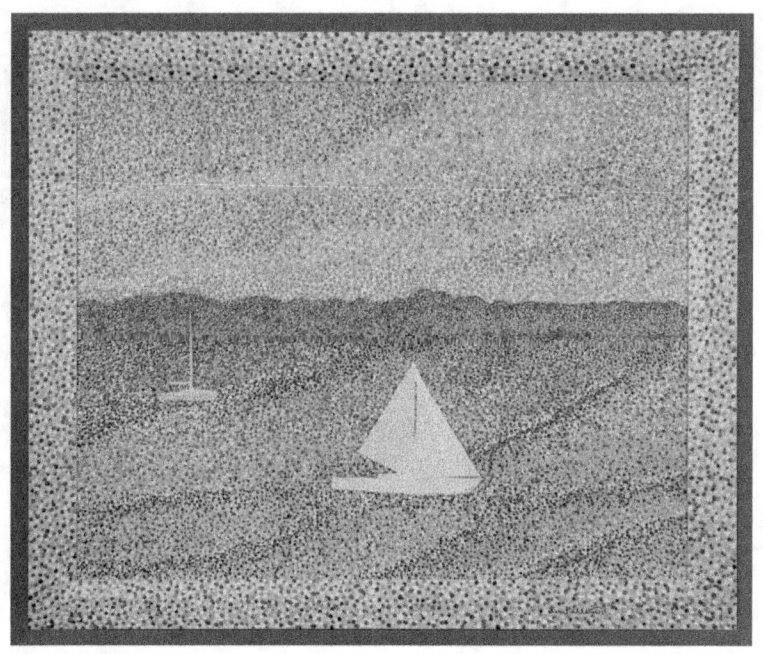

PART 4 NATURAL LIFE

Plate 21 Campsite 14" X 18",
acrylic on canvas board

The magnificent rough water, in effect a controlling force against the rocky cliff, pulls the eye into the scene. The fact that everything is volatile is shown by the quick and nervous touches of paint that create the trees and plants, and also by the indeterminate shapes of the clouds. The passion and energy of the bush transcends the ideal composure of the forest, reinterpreting it with a pantheistic lyricism. In Campsite there is the suggestion of the coolness of the water, the texture of leaves and grass, with the contrast of the hard rock surfaces as all are presented in an Impressionistic manner.

Impressionism is probably the most frequently used term in reference to painting. As a result, it suffers irregularities of meaning. Theoretically, the artist is concerned with the rendering of light playing over surfaces – without regard for the weights, tensions and volumes of forms, or of their linear contour. Feeling and content is subordinated to the perceptual study of light: its vibration, refraction and reflection, as well as its composition of pure hues, and of the contrast between warm and cool colours. Detail is sacrificed to the overall impact. One resulting technique is to spontaneously put down patches of pure colour.

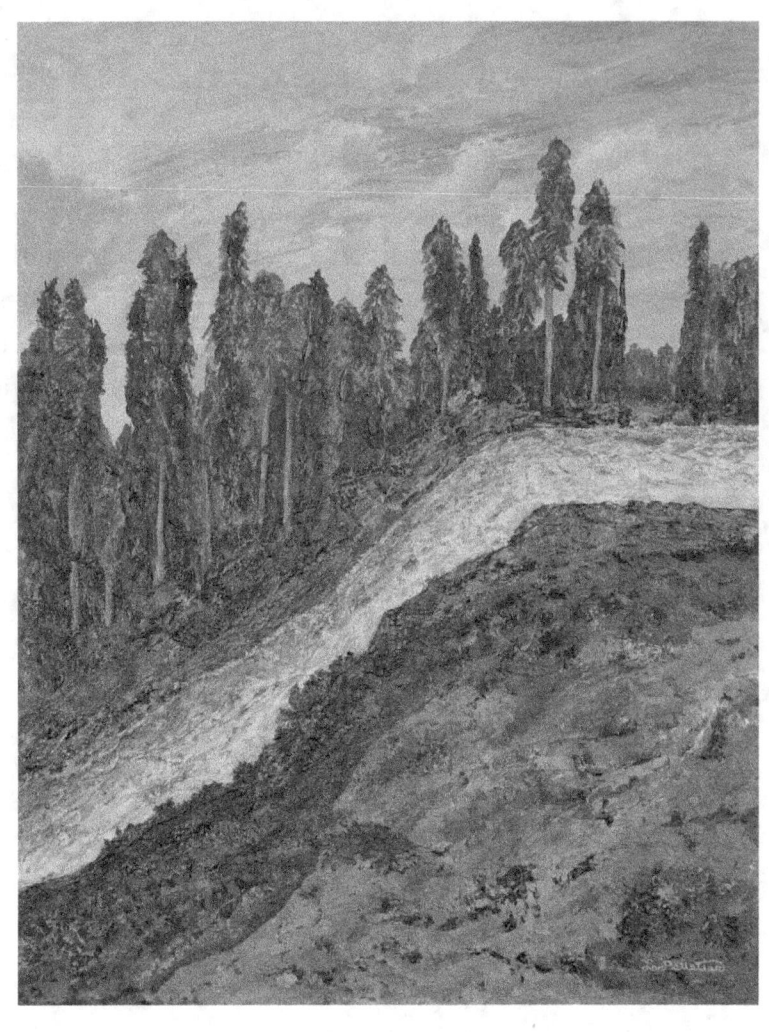

Plate 22 The Neuschwanstein Castle of Mad Ludwig II of Bavaria 14" X 18", acrylic on canvas board

Painted after viewing this on a 1999 trip, this work evokes the "fairy tale" perception of architecture that was the goal of its designer. Although the scene represented in the painting is in a Primitive style, its lyrical quality makes it contemporary in expression. There is a juxtaposition of colour values, similar to those used by the Impressionistic movement. However, the tonal organization of the picture was developed in a series of preparatory drawings. The subject matter is organized by light and dark contrast, as warm and cool spots of colour.

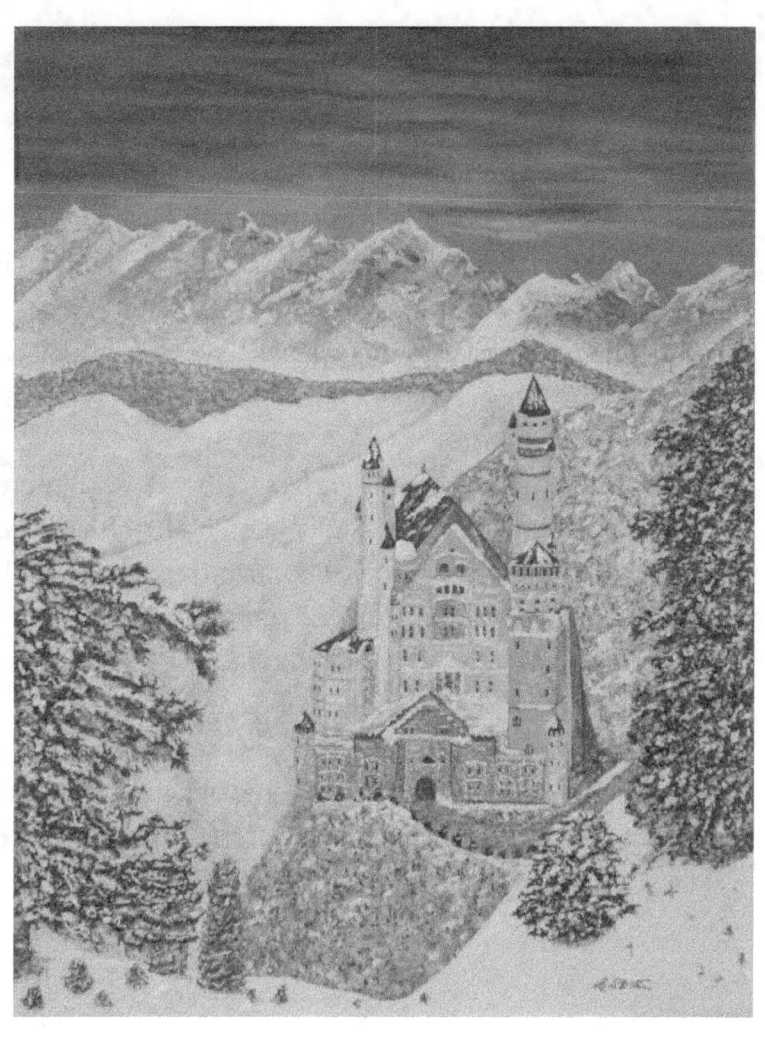

Plate 23 Leeds Castle 14" X 18",
acrylic on canvas board

Painted from sketches made after viewing this castle on a 1998 trip to England, this work replicates a medieval style of painting. The minute attention to details (the oxen cart, high doors and offset architectural perspective) is similar to the ancient style. The lack of outdoor atmosphere and the pretentious view of nature were also common.

Classical Art generally refers to the art – sculptural and architectural – of the Greek nation of the fifth century B.C. and to Roman imitations. It is characterized by dignity and reserve, and by the idealized representation of the human form. The term has come to mean all subsequent art that conforms to the models and the rules of these antique examples, especially as being the opposite of contemporary art works. By both emulating the medieval subject matter, and using a medieval style, this painting of Leeds Castle could be defined as Classical Art.

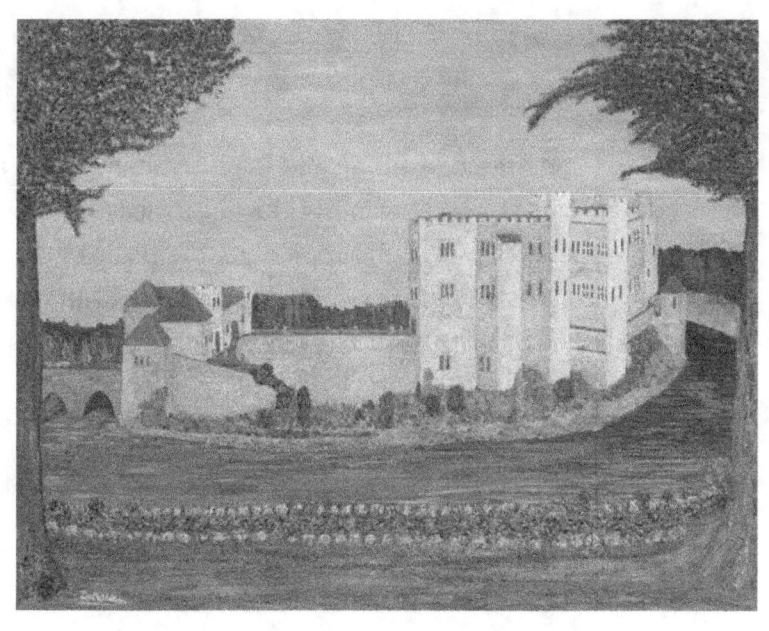

Plate 24 Cubic Fields, Tourouvre, France 20" X 24", acrylic on canvas

At one time Cubism moved from an analytical to a more synthetic period. This more flowing style is presented here. The reason for painting the fields of France was not significant to the visual area, but rather was a point of painting near the initiation of Cubism as a movement.

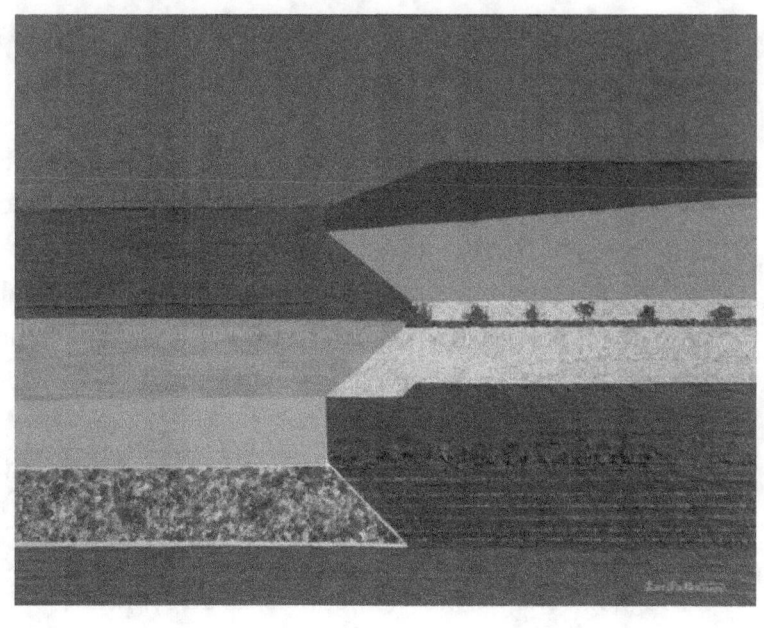

Plate 25 A Horse Of Course 20" X 24",
acrylic on canvas

Cubism is an attempt to solve the plastic problems involved in the relationships of two dimensional space to the illusion of three dimensional form. It deals with structural qualities in which objects are broken into small facets or planes as in Analytical Cubism. This includes the analysis of both form and volume. The form is decomposed, simplified to a geometric shape and reassembled from multiple points of view in an abstractly organized space. With the addition of increased spontaneity or with the arbitrary building up of objects through flat shapes, it is sometimes called Synthetic Cubism.

In this piece, there is a consistent geometrical structuralisation of the subject. Cubism is art that deals primarily with form. Cubism leads into such movements as Orphic Cubism, Constructivism and Futurism.

Orphic Cubism is also called Orphism and is a development of Cubism. In it, the spectrum colours of Fauvism are used in large, contrasting patches. The forms are abstracted to take on a secondary role.

Simultaneism is a later form of Orphic Cubism and is distinguished by a simultaneous contrast of colours. The term can apply to superimposed images presented in the same painting, or to descriptions of an object's various aspects, or as it might be seen from differing points of view.

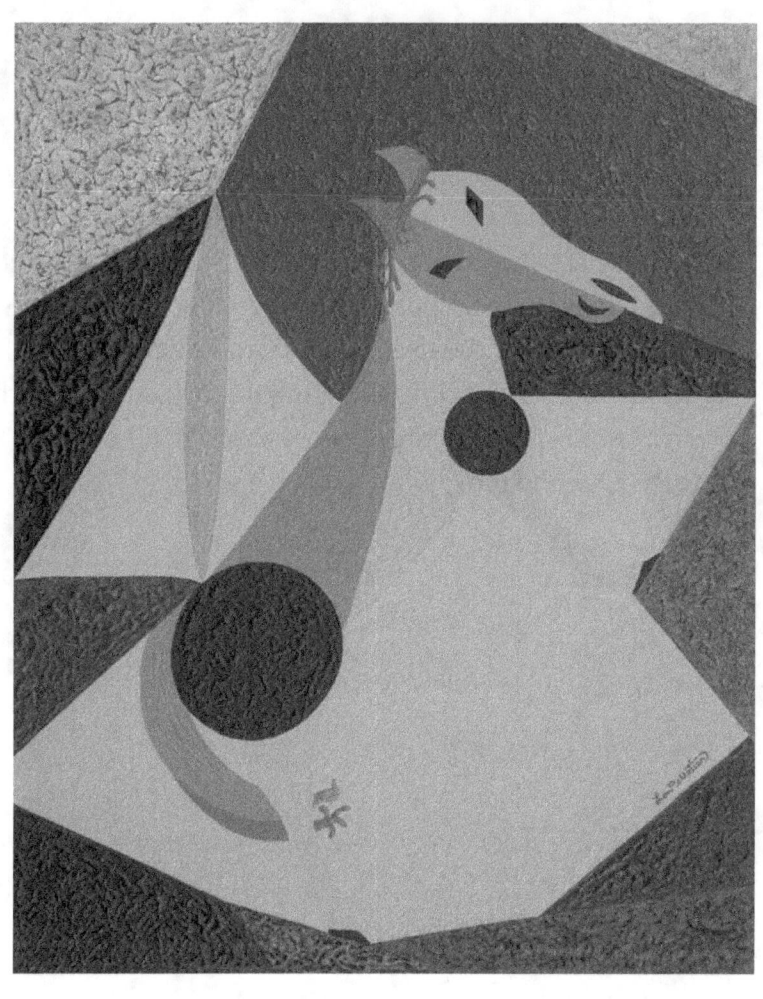

Plate 26 Three Coloured Horses 20" X 24", acrylic on canvas

Fauvism was initially the name describing the style of a group of painters who displayed rebellion against academic art and Impressionism. Les Fauves means "wild beasts" in French. Complementary, but pure and irrational, colours are used. Fauvist works will show flattened space and simplified design with examples such as a blue cow, or as in these two-dimensional horses in green, blue and red.

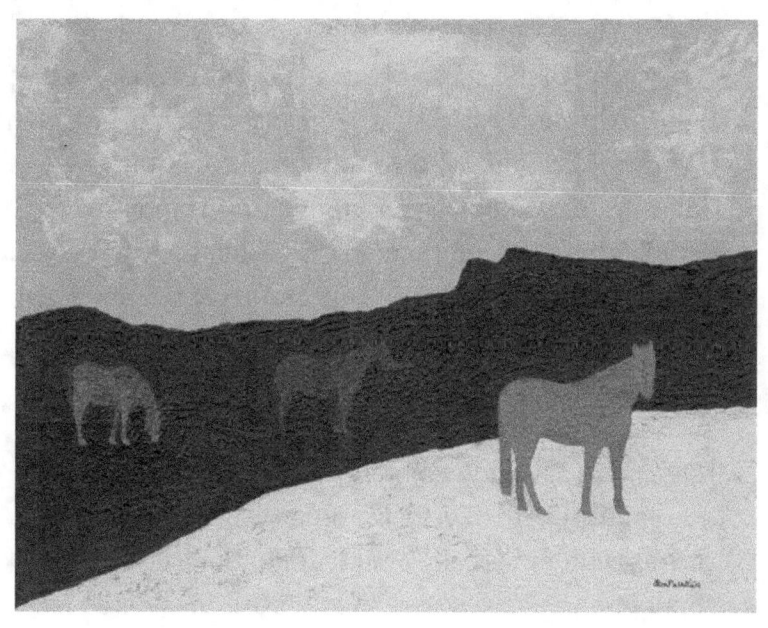

The evolution of art movements led to pure abstraction in the sense of subject (matter) on longer being relevant. Abstract Expressionism is a movement in abstract art that relies on a spontaneous, intuitive approach to painting and sculpture, with emphasis on the act of painting rather than on the result. As a movement, it reaffirmed a belief in the importance of the physical activity involved in creating a painting.

This often resulted in a dramatization of the accidentals of drip, dribble and splash; it is sometimes referred to as Action Painting. Just as the pure psychic automatism of the Surrealist poets was intended to express (either verbally or in writing) the true functions of thought, the uncontrolled splashes are considered an extension of the painter's inner being. It is pure aesthetics dictated in the absence of all control exerted by reason, or other outside aesthetic or moral preoccupations

The primacy of the visible objective is lost and with it all foresight in the construction of the surface. Rather than the rational elaboration of the image through the exercise of observation, one has the emergence of unconscious forces that the subject does not control, allowing them rather than the artist to direct this hypnotic state of non-premeditation.

This then became Nonobjective Expressionism.

PART 5 NON-OBJECTIVE EXPRESSION

Within non-objective works, colour is dominant, this being within limited local colour in all of the works. Geometry comes more to the surface, as there is nothing arbitrary about the placing of these many shapes. These paintings are evocative of a feeling for line or colour as the chief means of creating form as well as showing intrinsic calligraphic possibilities. These non-objective works have left the painterly approach to the non-ending problem of rendering a three-dimensional subject on a two-dimensional plane.

They are art works dealing with forms – which is a life often communicated by a subject but recreated in a separate object on the painting surface. I hope to have created a reaction to life expressed with tensions, distortion and contrasts, in form, space and colour. When subject matter is used, for example a still life, it is simply a pretext of lines and colour and nothing more comes from it at the first contemplation. These works are a departure from this process, and as they are not a rendering of an object, they become a reaffirmation of the creation process – often resulting in a dramatization of the chance, or a spontaneous creation of emotion.

Abstraction is a relative term and it is present in all painting. Abstract elements of line, shape, colour and space are used in representing any recognizable object, when it is created on a two-dimensional surface. The art of painting or creating new structures out of elements, which have not been borrowed from the visual sphere, only exists in non-objective works.

Many of these paintings show the sensation of colour alone as being both form and subject. Communication of emotion is the only goal. Most of the works are not titled for the specific reason that the title may dictate that which is perceived, rather than that which is painted. I have been one of the first of many, within the group of painters of the abstract, who have opted out of using titles as captions - within this type of contemporary communication. The abstraction of art may then be within the "mind's eye" of the beholder, and left at that.

Plate 27 Climax - 24" X 30", oil on canvas

This work represents a style and methodology that I developed in the late 1960's. During this period of popular Psychedelic Art, I preferred to build up an individual style of handling paint on canvas. Using a 24" X 36" or 30" format, these paintings were popular in contemporary office environments. Other works of a similar popularity were imitations of the styles of Jackson Pollock, Jean-Paul Riopelle and others. The whole composition is animated by contrasts and unified by analogies. This is created by the close knitting of lines and brushed planes, within a very tight colour scale.

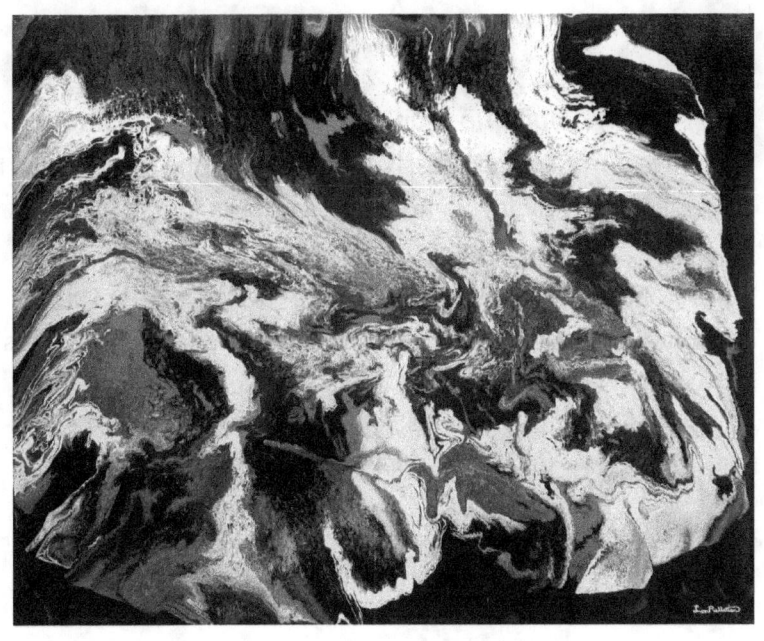

Plate 28 Blues - 24" X 36", oil on canvas

The build-up is an orchestration of form and colour, and is purposely expressive. As the painting progresses, I seek intuitively for an arrangement of colours that will express specific feelings. The whole composition is animated by contrasts and unified by analogies. This is created by the close knitting of lines and brushed planes, within a very tight colour scale. Abstraction is a relative term, and is actually present in all painting. The abstract elements of line, shape, colour and space are used in representing any recognizable concrete object in some way on a two-dimensional surface, rather than creating it with its actual texture or rendering it three-dimensionally.

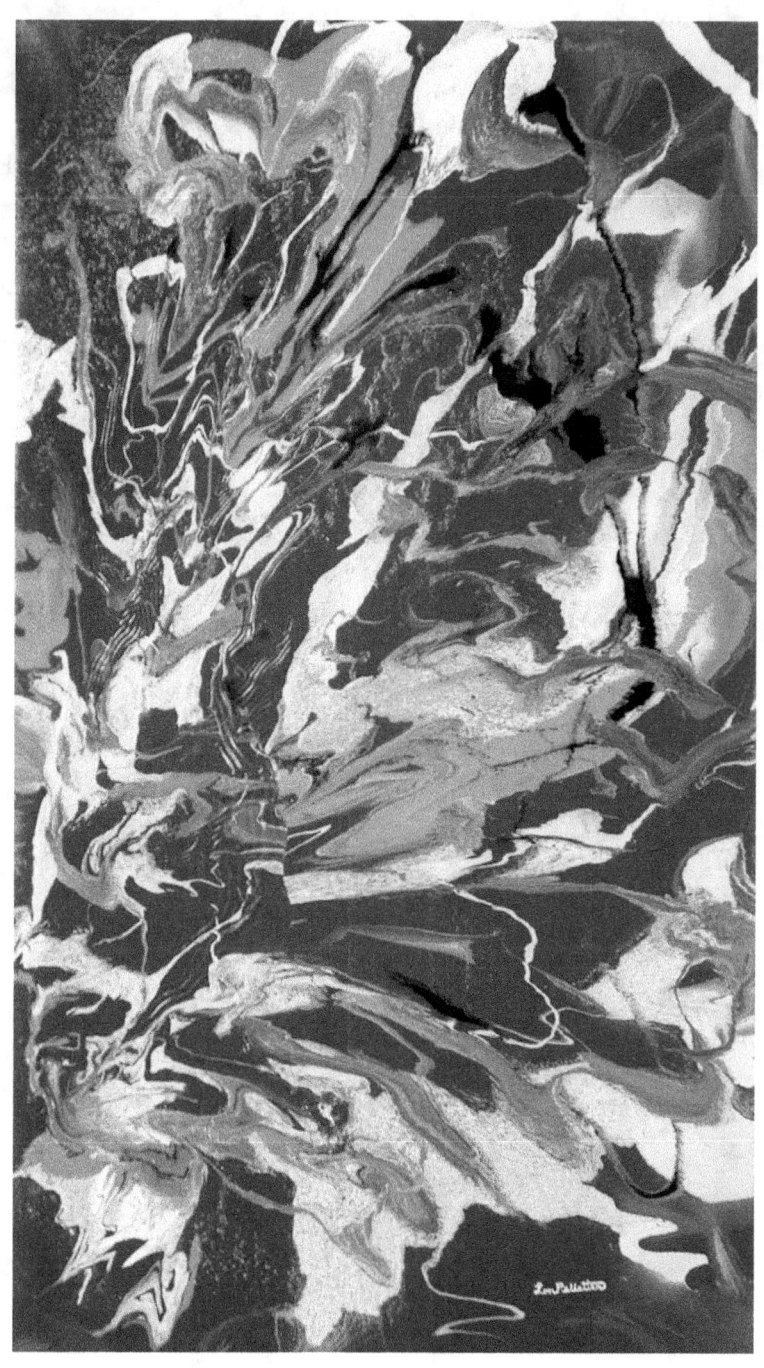

Plate 29 Floating - 24" X 36", oil on canvas

As an art dealing primarily with forms, when the form is realized it is there to live its own life – a life that is communicated by the subject, but recreated in the object. The departure from a coastal mountain scene may be evident. The geometrical idiom is gradually modified and replaced by freer and more cursive forms, an iconography of individual taste, but art that may still be viewed as possibly serene or comforting.

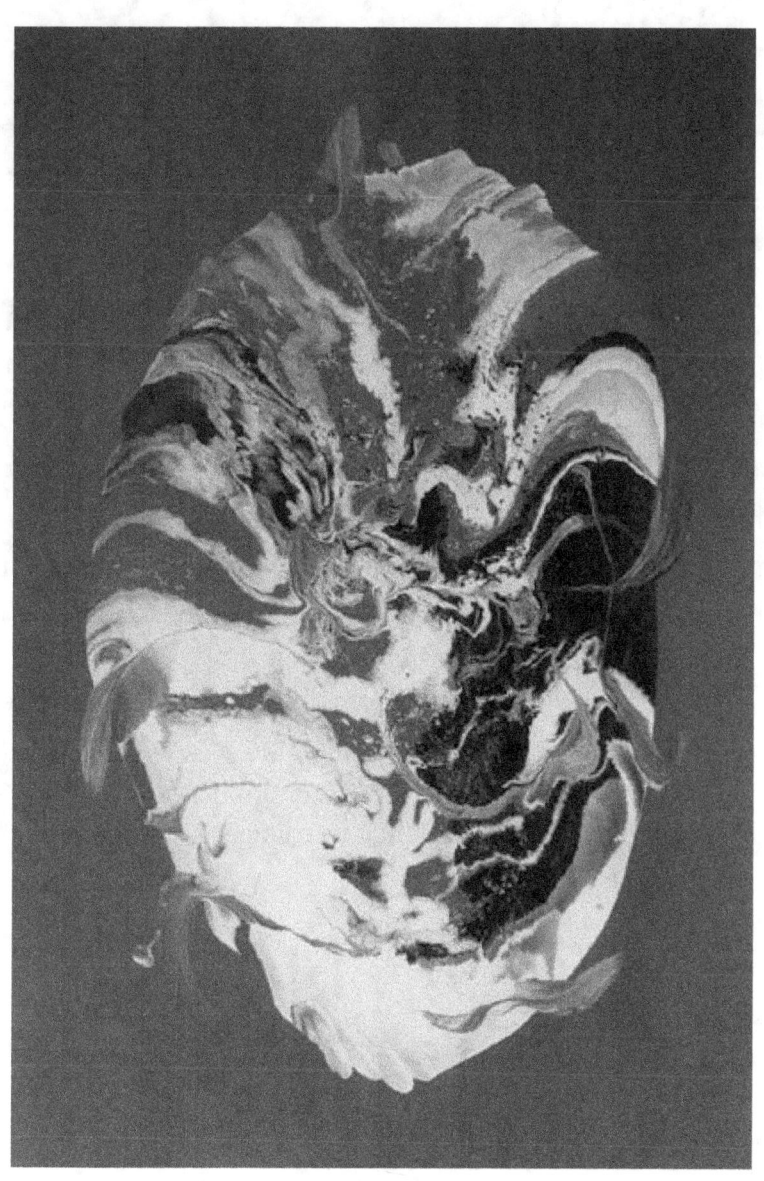

Plate 30 Warm Evocation 24" X 36", oil on board

Painted in 1972, this is one of approximately three hundred works of this genre sold to various corporations in the early 1970's. These works are still held in corporate collections primarily in Western Canada. This work shows the construction of forms out of the pure elements of line, light and dark, warm colour and texture, as opposed to naturalistic representation. Pure abstraction is non-representational and non-objective. It does not depict any recognizable visual object. The style often contains geometric shapes, but as is shown here, it is sometimes utilizes embryonic forms or even amorphous creations.

While the painting may seem related to Splash Art styles, it is set apart by its meaning and by its process. The painting took five days to complete and was done in a very meticulous and thought-out painting application. In this case, Automatism resorts systematically to the dictates of the unconscious rather than to chance.

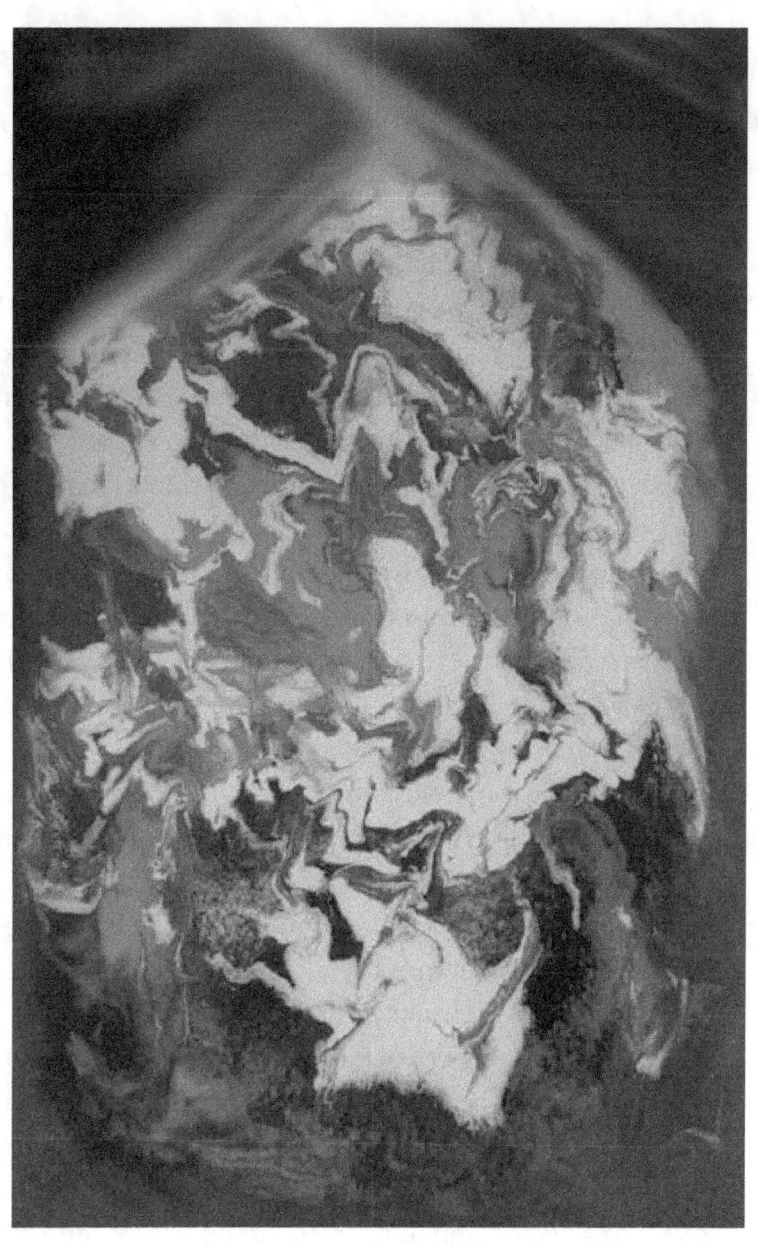

Plate 31 Tashism For Lunch 14" X 20", oil on board

My tashism works are held in collections in Canada and France. I had studied the specific art technique in Paris, France, during the sixties. Tachism is a style of painting in which colour is applied in splotches or blots (taches) of colour. The composition is alive with punctuations of vivid colour, often with each brush stroke being independent of other small touches. The taches are placed on the canvas spontaneously and by chance; however, planned composition of color (colour) may be a part of the process.

As is often the case, an artist can forget to save one work of each style (from each period of development) for his own collection. Having reflected on this – of not having any examples of Tachism left in my personal collection – I created this work in 2000. I had painted and sold internationally thirty works of Tachism in 1970 and 1971.

Care was given to arranging the motif, and plotting campaigns of form and colour. During the painting the touches of paint, tonal masses, and linear patterns were modified, and sometimes transformed, until the complex and dynamic relationship was resolved.

The Paris School of Painters originally referred to a group in Paris during the late Middle Ages. They painted in the candlelight style of the "Illuminators." While the term has lost its specific reference to any single group, it still refers to any contemporary group of the sixties, centred at Paris, France, typically painting in these contemporary styles - within which I qualified.

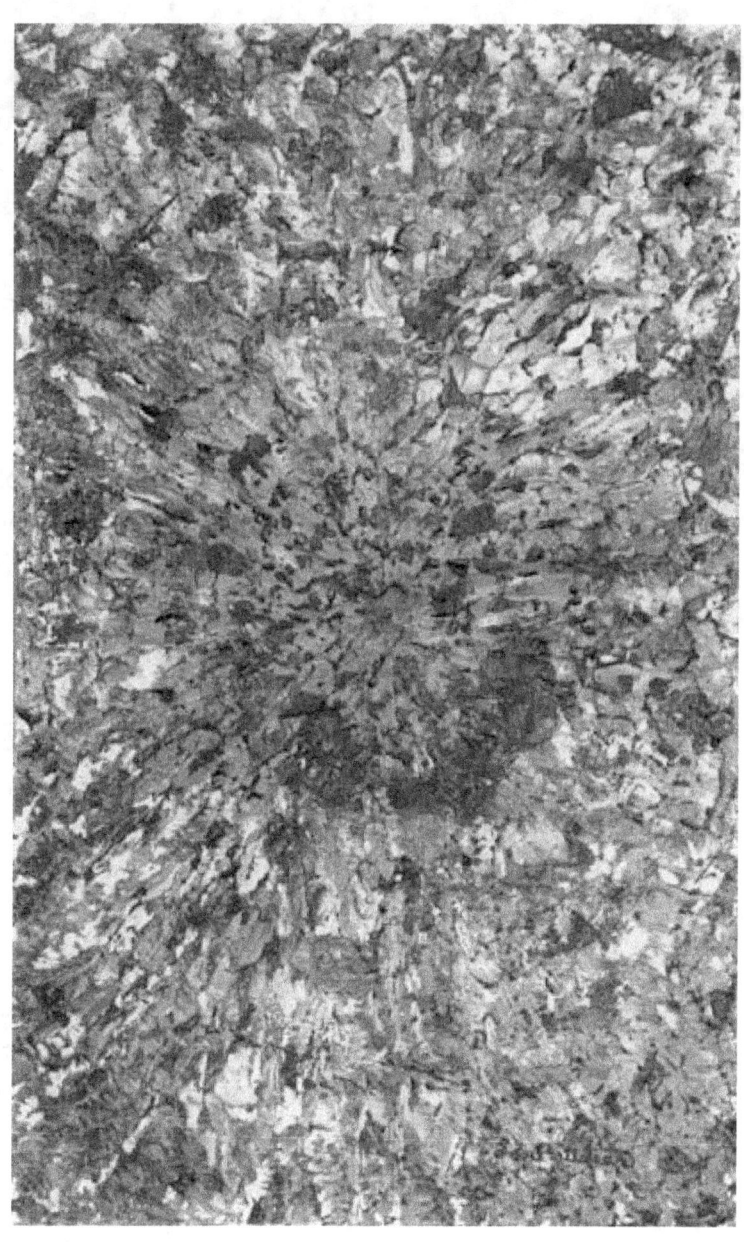

Plate 32 For Mondrian 24" X 30", acrylic on canvas board

Geometric Abstraction is a nonrepresentational style of painting that uses two-dimensional geometric shapes, rather than shapes of perspective. The subordination of composition to geometrical form is not a new idea, and it has often been presented in Modern Art. The Persians focused on this quest and type of Nonobjective Expressionism of symbolism many centuries ago.

This painting does not purely imitate the group of painters known as the Constructivists; however, it is very much inspired by them. They believed that art needed to turn away from nature and seek inspiration from within the artist's mind. This art forms questions as to why universal beauty should continue to appear in art under a veiled or covert form, and why nature seemed to remain essential in any search for pure beauty. Symmetry was to be excluded and rhythm adhered to, with a sense of equilibrium achieved by straight lines and angles.

Opposing elements were required, so that a difference in size and colours could become equal in value. Two sorts of equilibrium in art exist. The first is the static balance and the second is dynamic equilibrium. Abstract art is a concrete expression of such a structured vitality; it often evolves into being dominated by its rhythmical vitality.

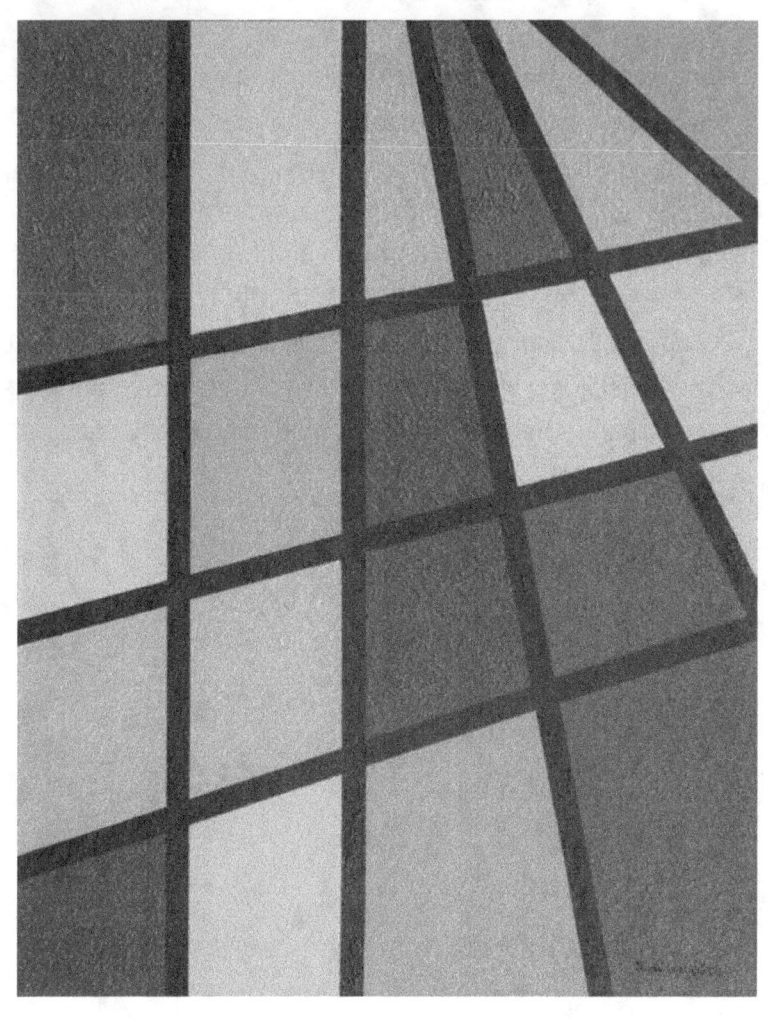

Plate 33 Desire 20" X 30", oil on canvas

Cloisonnism is a style of painting that derives its name from cloisonné enamelling, a process of filling in metal-outlined areas with enamel. Painted in 2004, the painting style consists of flat decorative areas of colour that are strongly outlined or pasted in. These patches of expression are symbolic of the attempt to fragment it for analysis. Stylistically, a structure is given to the painting by the considered relationship of its constituent colours. I used the element of composition itself to define the expression of feelings.

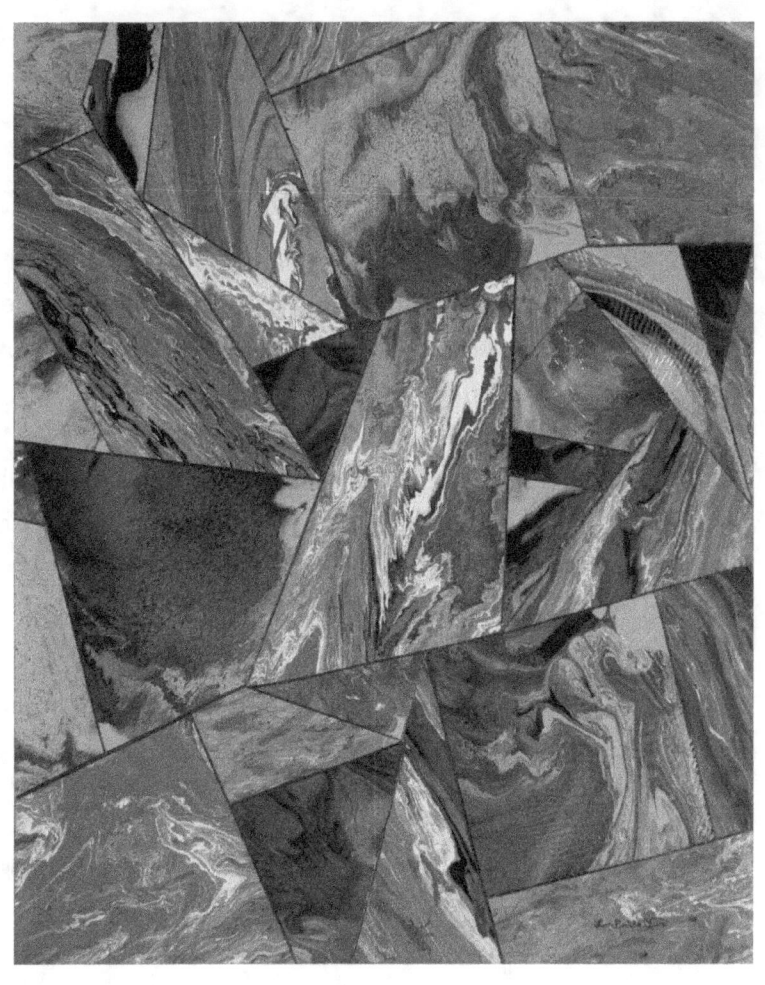

Plate 34 Untitled 1 - 20" X 36", oil on canvas

Lines seem to fluctuate and represent not only movement, but also purpose and growth. Colours are associated not only with the human emotions of joy, sadness, and so on, but also to the significance of emotive aspects of external environment. Yellow is earthy and here it is somewhat is upward sky. In this manner, yellow is also brash and importunate and as such it invariably may actual upset individual observers. Blue is pure and infinite and it suggests external peace. In both colours, with their variations of hue, the earth around us becomes symbolic as an orchestrated form.

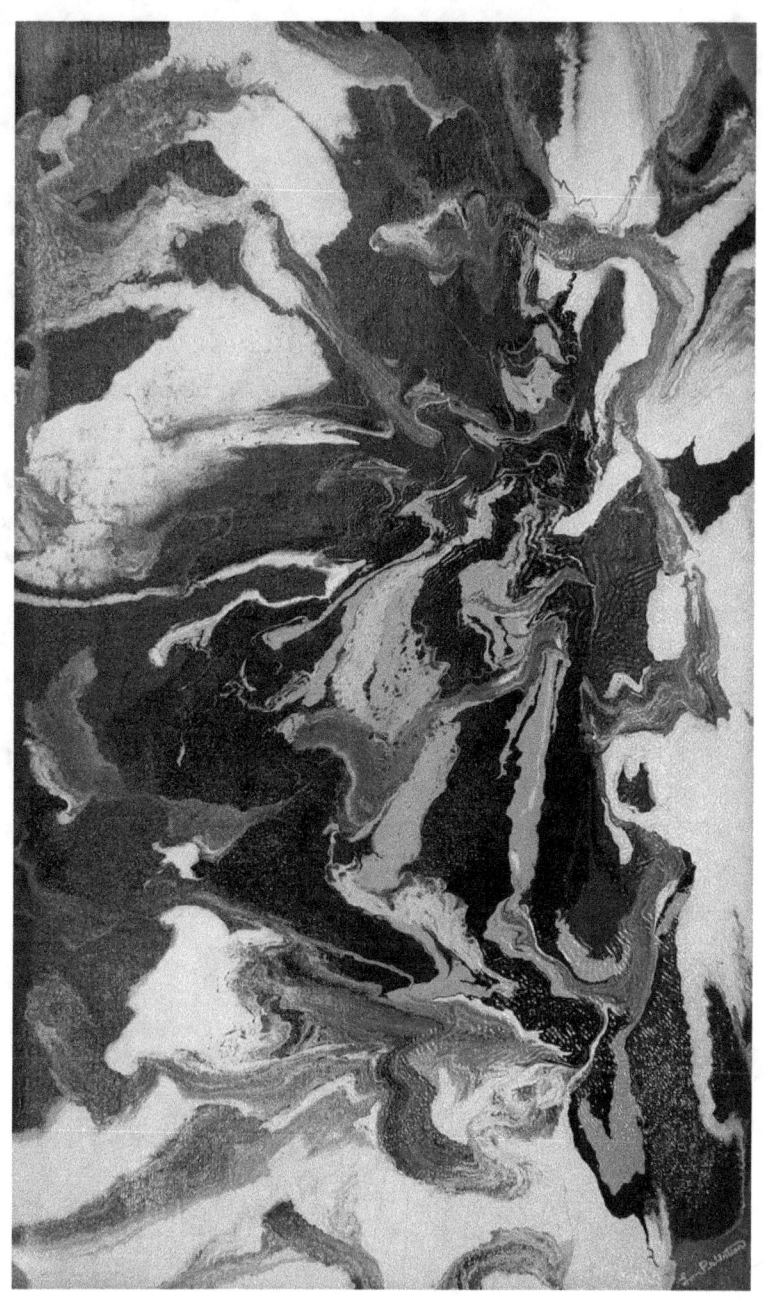

Plate 35 Untitled 2 - 20" X 32", acrylic on board

The lyrical imagination and innovations in light and colour are used to attain harmonies of colour to construct form. The semi-geometrical, almost classical composition of this work, suggests a relationship that is almost a prelude to geometrical construction. The basic concern was not a visual realism, but a structural pattern composed of flat geometrical areas of textured or shaded hues. It is a dissociation of design and form, with an analytical activity and dissociation of contour suggesting movement. Suprematism is a completely abstract geometric form of Cubism, and this work relates to the Suprematist perceptions of rendering. The movement emphasized precision, clarity, and the impersonal technological influences of modern life. The spirit of this work is the outcome of an involved intellectual process. With the juxtaposition created within the composition, geometric surfaces have replaced volume.

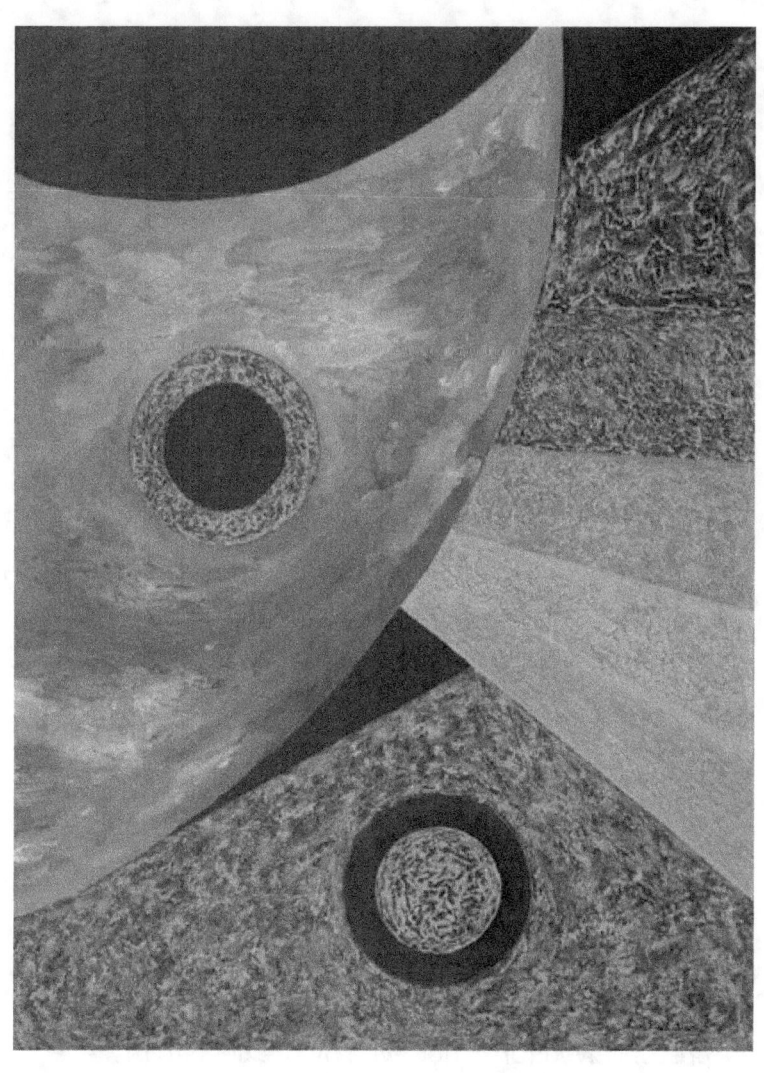

Plate 36 Pink For Christie 24" X 36", oil on canvas

Painted in 1981. When my daughter Christie was still a preschooler, she wanted her own artwork. Here then is a work that was done for her in the style of Splash Art. It has been said that man is enabled by abstract aesthetic contemplation to achieve conscious unity with the universal.

This was one such attempt. An examination of Splash Art suggests signs of loss of optical control, while painting abstracted lines. When painting in this manner, the path the paint follows across the canvas has much in common with the gesture of a man who gropes his way in the dark. There is nothing pre-planned about the route taken. It is led from one point of the object to another. The painter only sees this by itself, with no relation to any other point to which the paint will eventually make its way. Within the painting, the smaller units of thinly painted colour have become free agents, acting more individually. These staccato lines, which sometimes coincide with a colour plane, serve to strengthen the overall colour structure.

The artist's hand is guided then, not by any preconceived form, nor even by the need to make connections between the different points or stages of the drawing. The gesture always remains unfinished, and the effect of the composition only arrives after the fact. The artist doesn't decide on the direction of this journey, nor on its length or the guiding thread he must follow through the dark to the completed form. Rather, he follows a movement of return towards an indistinct form where the visual encounters the unknown. The drawing does not derive from an already constituted subject that finds direct expression, nor is it guided to a previously determined point of completion.

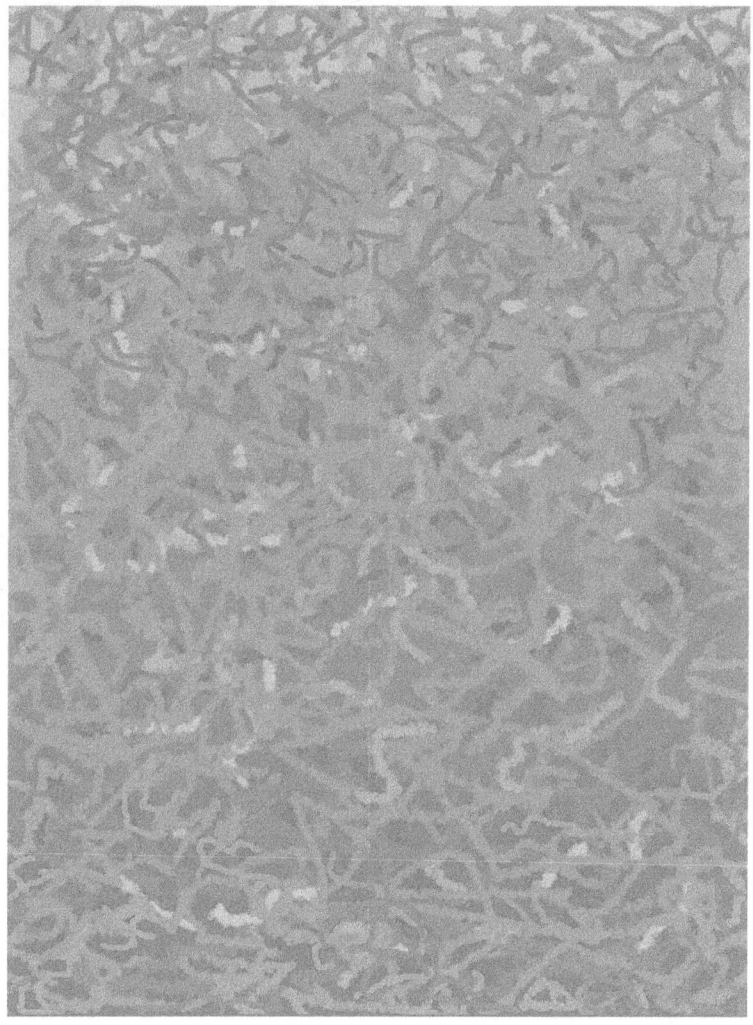

PART 6 ABSTRACTION EXPRESSED

When subject matter is used, for example a still life, it is simply a pretext of lines and colour and nothing more comes from it. These works are a departure from this process, however they are a rendering of an object, unlike Nonobjective Expressionism.

Plate 37 Subservient Man 16" X 30",
acrylic on canvas board

Dada is the only movement that may be considered anti-rational and anti-aesthetic. Unfortunately, it was a type of Nihilism. The Dada movement was motivated by disillusionment and disgust with social values of the time, to the point that it even rejected being accepted as a part of its contemporary art scene. It did however, anticipate Surrealism with its often seen desire to outrage, shock or generally exasperate with its choices of unique subject matter. These attitudes re-emerged in Pop Art, Psychedelic Art and Happenings as a form of expressing non-conventionalism.

As the goal was to be evocative of a male being in the *rut* of consistently serving I was not concerned with the male form. Minimalism is used for the same reason. Outlines are after Matisse, the "father" of minimalism.

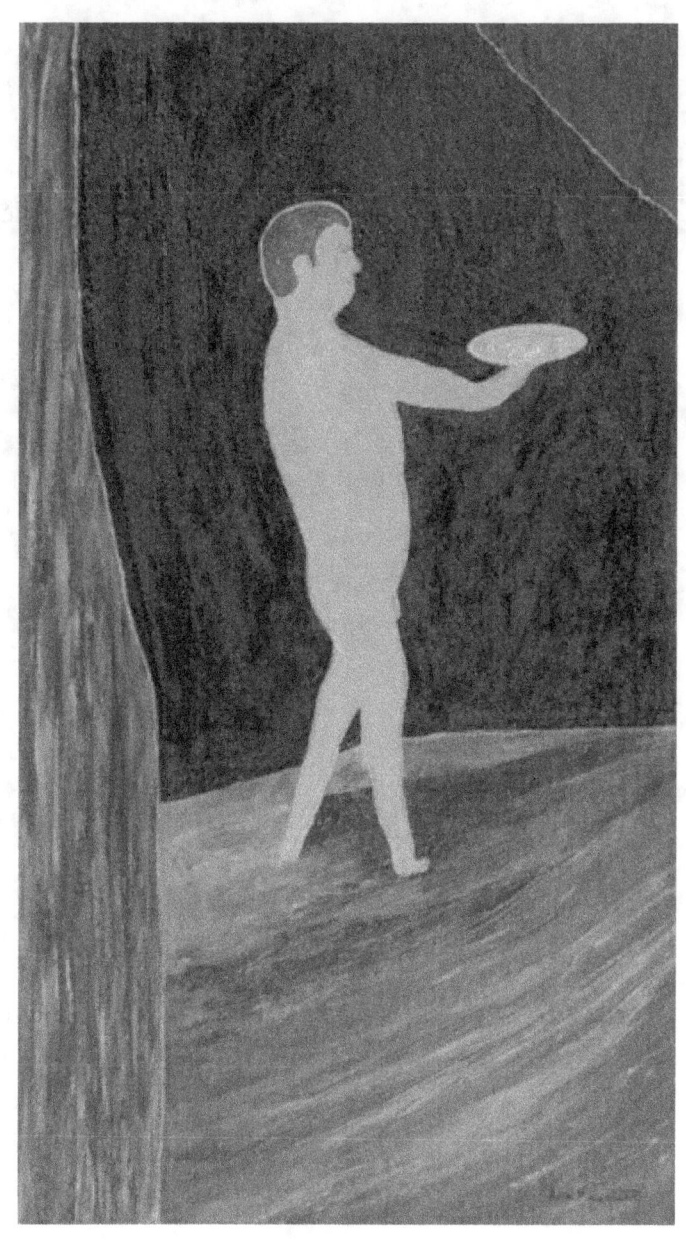

Plate 38 Storm's Break I - 20" X 28",
acrylic on board

Hard Edge is a term used to describe a style of abstract painting characterized by a precise geometrical division of planes and often uses pure colours. It is in antithesis to the lost-and-found or blended contours of the more painterly approach. Hard Edge follows the tradition of the De Styl movement and its principles of abstract geometric design. In the context of symbolic reference to sun, sea and sky, an objectivity has been added.

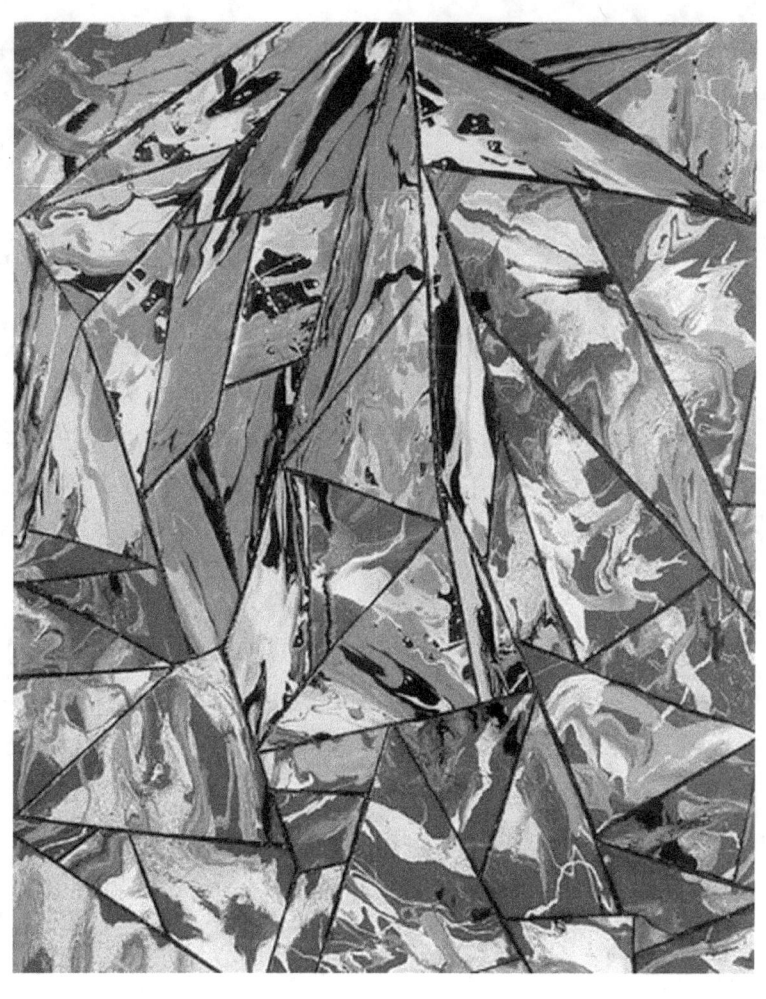

Plate 39 Storms Break II - 18" X 28",
acrylic on board

Neo-Plasticism is a movement founded by the
Dutch painter and architect, Mondrian. Simple and
geometric in style, it was applied to other forms of design
besides painting, mainly through association with
practitioners of De Styl. It lends itself to theories of colour
relationships with its evocation of dimension and depth.
"The Style" or De Styl applied the principle of geometric
abstraction to both the fine and applied arts and its
theories were advocated by the Bauhaus Group in
Germany. However with the original manifestos of De Stijl,
it was declared that painting must be made to submit to
the horizontal-vertical order, which excludes the diagonal
and the curve. Colours were to be limited to the three
primary colours; the three non-colours of white, black and
gray were never to be included.

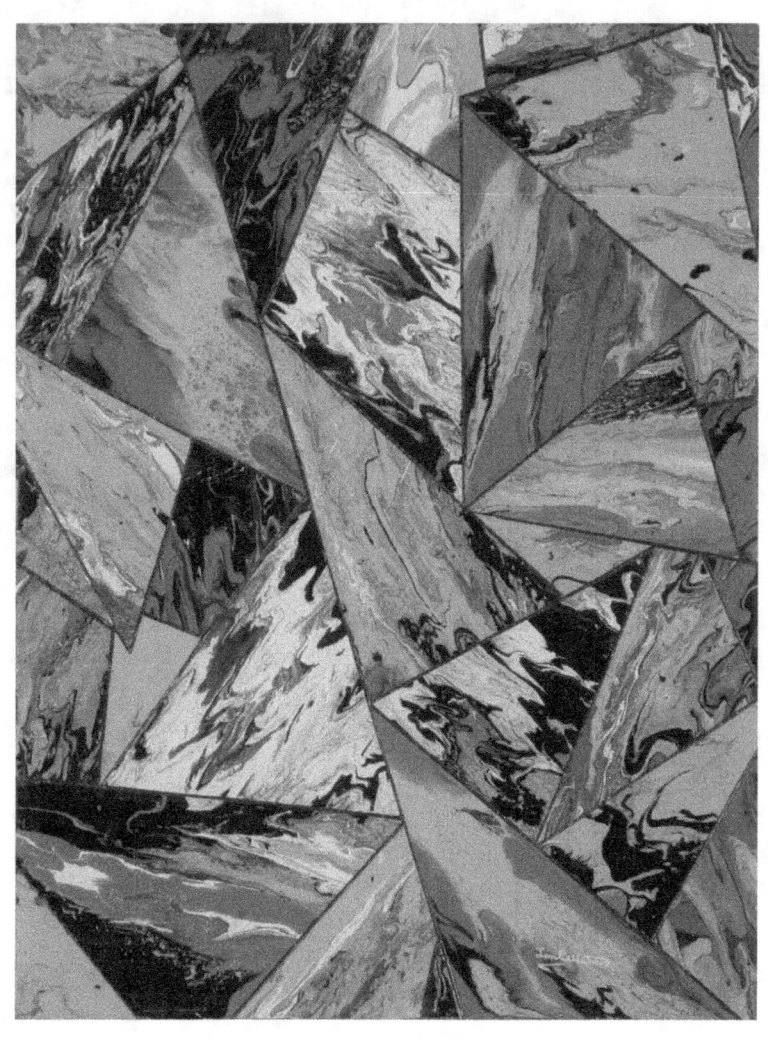

Plate 40 Storms Break III - 17" across, 24" on the diagonal and 1.5" deep, oil on canvas with inlaid cuttings

With a complete freedom of form, and being a seascape in an abstract sense, a unique dynamic is created with the intersecting of lines and many curvaceous colour patterns.

This work is completely non-objective, as there is no existing reference to a subject. Being a six-sided form it is a non-rectangular format, itself an integral part of its own design.

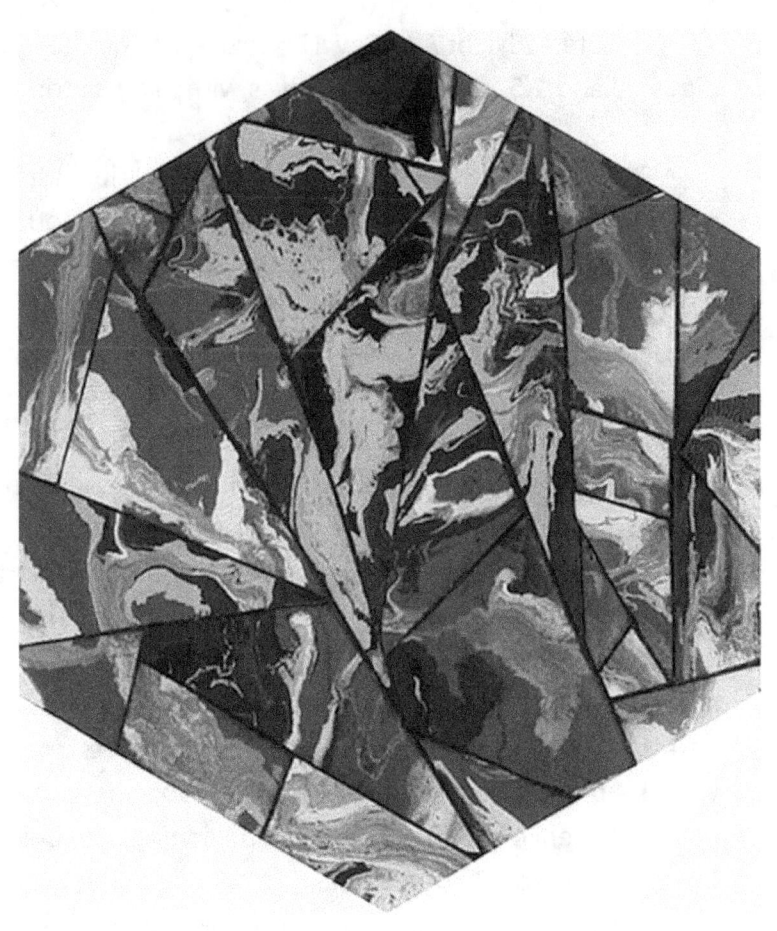

Plate 41 Night And Day 17" across, 24" on the diagonal and 1.5" deep, oil on canvas with inlaid cuttings

Hard Edge as being a term used to describe a style of abstract painting characterized by a precise geometrical division of planes and the often use of pure colours, does not apply here - even though there are common denominators to the formation of the composition. Such is the apparent illusion that the ongoing pursuits in art can in some way following the original manifestos of the classic movements. In actual fact it is quite impossible to follow these manifestos, as the initiating artists were prone to deviate into yet newer movements, within short periods of time. Even within this text, the categories of many Non-objective works through to an objective use of Abstract Expressionism are confused by the issue of presenting these three six-side works as a progression. It was as a progression that they originally evolved as paintings, hence they deviated from beginning with being forms related to a "storms break", to colour for the pure pleasure of its use, on to a black, white and gray study of the symbolic form of "night and day".

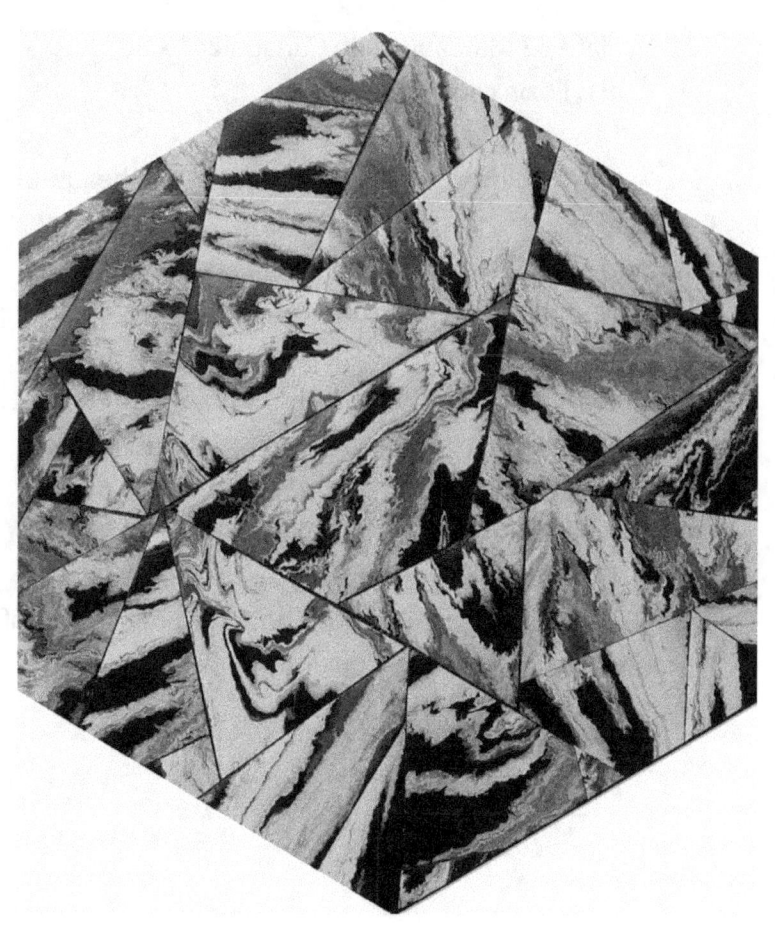

Plate 42 Ma Cabane au Canada 24" X 30",
acrylic on canvas

"My Cabin In Canada" was sung by the beautiful Canadian *chanteuse*, Line Renaud. It was on the Top Ten in France in 1949. Being in Paris, France, in 2005, and looking for an inspiration to paint a collage, finding this original piece of music was perfect. The words are dated in their references to our country, such that they are quite hilarious - leading to the *necessity* of my painting this work. The musical notations, as well as the lyrics, are shown in detail on the pasted collage.

The painting's composition is also comprised of Expressionist Symbolism. Subtly shown are the figures of a woman and a man, all on a quiet moonlit night.

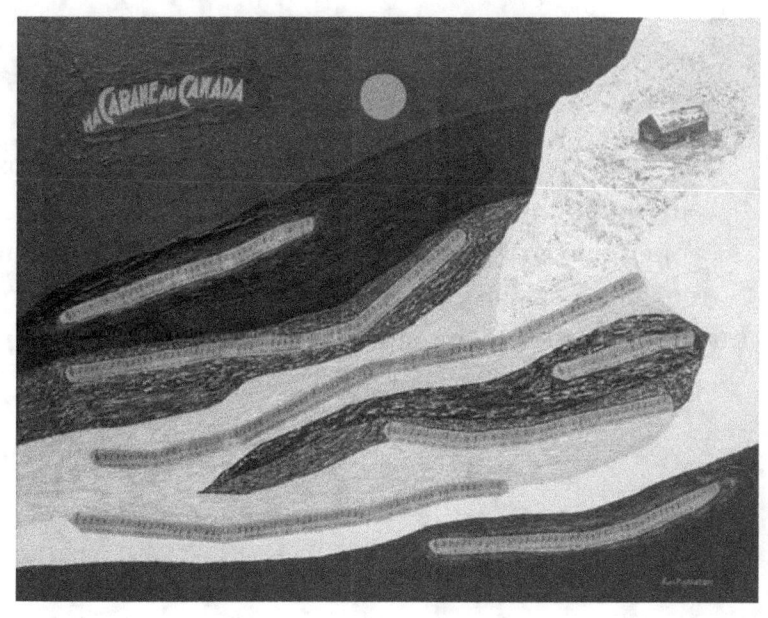

Plate 43 Singular Sorrow 24" X 30",
acrylic on canvas

The woman seems to be floating, and sits in a pose
I am sure I've seen many times. Despite that, the
composition is original, as is the quest for artistic value in
using this minimal number of lines. My attempts at
achieving an evocation of slow movement have been
influenced by observing the paintings of Matisse.

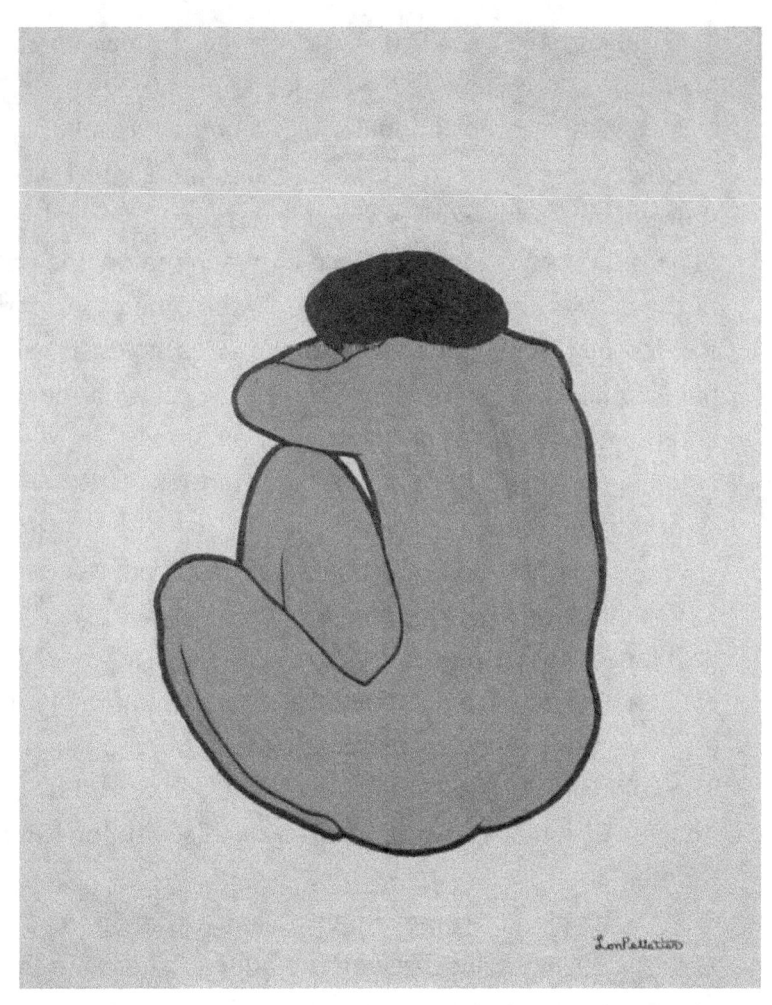

Plate 44 Fireball 20" X 24", acrylic on canvas

With a compositional use of a fireball traveling through outer space and having a devastating effect on these planets; this work is a focus on color. The premise is of a visual perception of balance between red on one-half of the canvas and a matching blue on the other. Even with a difference in size and color, the two sides nevertheless have equal value. This balance is creating color harmony, and the equilibrium is pre-eminently qualitative, as a balance of weights of color, not of dimensions or symmetry.

These last two works are a preview from a series of 125 paintings entirely focused on other galaxies and exoplanets - also presented on my web site. They are well-chosen within a presentation of the evolution of art.

A book of my art titled: "Galaxies - 65 Exoplanets" is in colour (color). It is available on Amazon.com and Amazon Europe. Four eBooks are available with the same theme.

The global art movement called "Outer Space Expressionism", coincides with the quote, "These are the paintings of other galaxies, not as illustrations, nor as science, but rather as aesthetic presentations.

It is this very exciting time that facilitates the normality of spacecapes as the painting of exoplanets. By not knowing their evolution nor being sure of the chemical makeup of their rocks, gases or liquids - there are no visual boundaries. *That initiates the fun of it all!*

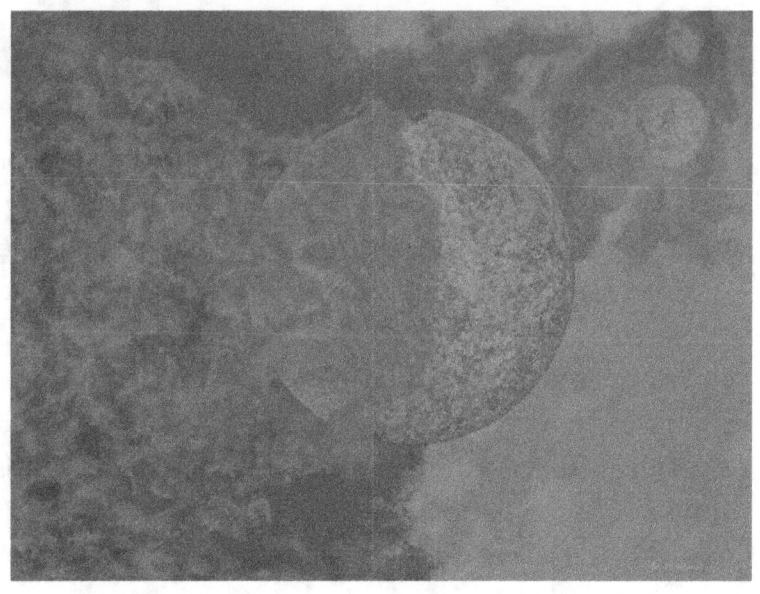

Astronomers have recently found 2,326 Earth-like planets having possible habitable zones around stars like our sun and 48 have been confirmed. The planet Kepler 22b is 2.4 times the size of Earth with a temperature averaging 22 C degrees. Three planets orbit a tiny red dwarf star KOI-961 with one named Gliese 581g, seeming identical to Earth. Proxima Centauri is a red dwarf star with a planet, Proxima b, that is 1.3 times the mass of Earth. The two Voyager space-probes have now passed out of our Sun's heliosphere's outer structure, therefore we are now actually exploring other solar systems physically. *It is a time when it is necessary that art joins in the portrayal of the beauty of science.*

Plate 45 GOLDEN NEBULA 36' X 36", oil on canvas

Often huge spirals of gas spin out from the stars with a pattern of glowing gas, all that is left from a major explosion. The colors correspond to glowing oxygen of blue and hydrogen and nitrogen as a reddish tint. Heavier elements may also evolve to be new planets. One rust colored planet has formed, with rust gases and dust having been released from it. Blue gases are set away from the blue planets; and gold gases are set apart from the gold planets. Even the green planet has its counterpart in the turquoise tints found nearby. Glowing debris from 11,000 years ago may still be viewed.

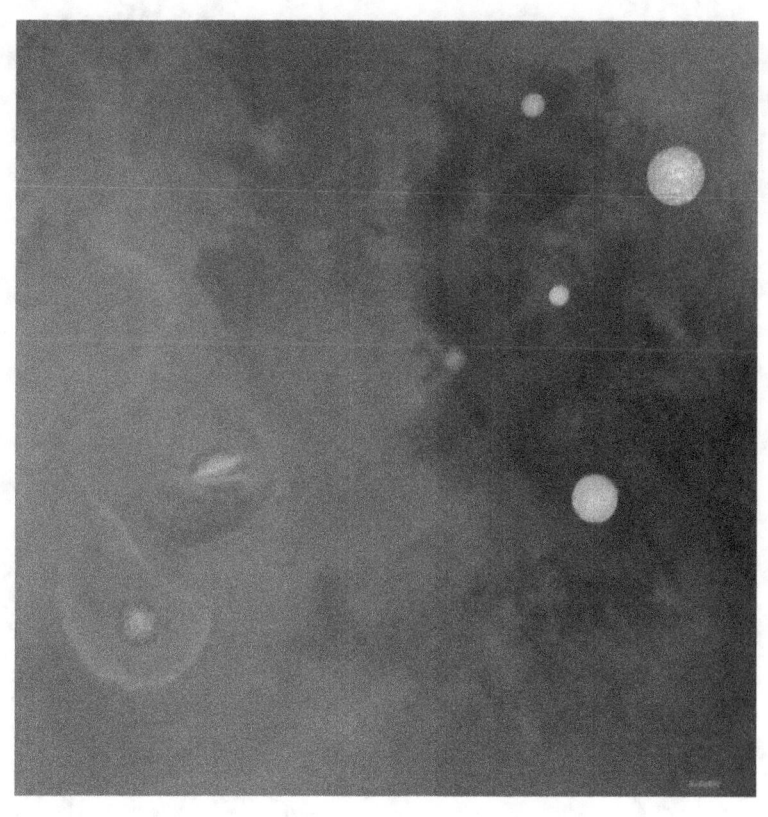

PART 7 ONE HUNDRED YEARS IN THE EVOLUTION

The origin of the word "Icon" is Greek, meaning an image or reflection. Icon was in that sense applied to the portative representations of holy personages, the saints of scenes taken from the Scripture. These wood panels in a style used one thousand years ago, were covered with a thin layer of gesso and powdered alabaster, which was hardened and polished. The artists worked in tempera, using raw yolk of egg diluted in rye beer as his medium. Their medium generally rendered the background in a gold leaf lain over priming made of red wine. It was from a time of the church, as the only patron of art, completely controlling by way of its creative theology.

The study of, and concern with the subject matter depicted – and its meaning in works of art – rather than with form, is "Iconography". This very bigoted but traditional manner of representing a subject was governed by fixed rules of symbolism. Although Iconography has a unique meaning in each applied field of study, it usually carries the context of that which is very narrow-minded, leaving no latitude for change. The evolution of computers has brought the word Icon into daily use. Contemporary art, even one thousand years later, has not changed in the artist's quest to render both symbolism and beauty.

Painting is not merely a rendering of the already visible, but it is a quest for communication by the artist working within various art movements – to make visible.

Those movements then define the work of art. Groups of individuals consistently became clustered, as single schools of thought within a particular era. Through the terminology of "isms" we are able to grasp the numerous styles and techniques, and thus an evocation of the world's metaphysical environment, and thus realize the unique social significance of art. The study of these movements reveals not just a study of painting, but perhaps offers a gauge by which to contemplate the complexity of religion, of science, and of bigotry. Mankind has always been mirrored by artists of each epoch. The following summaries also relate to twentieth century art movements that have influenced my works. I have listed these groups of artists chronologically. Evolution often crisscrossed both internationally and within the groups themselves - the new direction stated existed only in the first volatile period of the movement's emergence.

Generic terms from the world of art are also included, although no attempt has been made to make the descriptions anything more than executive summaries. Most importantly, this is a summary of the evolution of art. For that reason the use of approximate ten-year periods presents the more logical approach. The focus is only on Western European Culture in general, and on painting specifically.

However, most of these terms apply to literature, sculpture, dance and all that may be said to be evocative of an artistic state of mind. Classical Art generally refers to the art, both sculptural and architectural, of the Greek nation of the fifth century B.C. and to Roman imitations. It is characterized by dignity and reserve, and by the idealized representation of the human form. The term has come to mean all subsequent art that conforms to the models and the rules of these antique examples, these being the opposite of contemporary art works where feeling is the paramount solution to the rendering of that which is considered beauty.

Exemplifying the highest principals or the latter Classical period, innovations in painting with oils led to works with incredible detail.

Neo-Classicism was a style that appeared during the eighteenth and nineteenth centuries as a severe, moralistic and conscious imitation of the Roman antique. It is a tight, linear and intellectual style in its use of precise detail. One possible recent use of this conceptualization in art is the focus on paintings that "look just like a camera took the picture". This remark is typical of that being made by members of the unsuspecting public in their own quest for paintings – ones that are not art – by any definition. Romanticism was a movement that embodies poetic imagination and a passionate concern with feeling. Emotional colour was lavishly used; however, revival of Renaissance quest for detail was part of this movement. Neo-Romanticism was the name given to rather over-sentimental type of paintings which exhibit dreamlike nostalgic quality. It may also be called "Neo-Humanistic".

As a rejection against the "Neo-Classicists and Romantics", the Realists included writers, and concerned themselves with the realities of the time. The movement is an effort to depict the actual as it exists and as it is apprehended by the senses.

Realism differs from Naturalism in that Realism focuses on stressing the convincing, without minute detail – rather than the particular as it is used in Naturalism. Evocation of reality is their mutual quest. Often called the democratic art, Realism avoids the picturesque and the sentimental and states fact with detachment. The literal meaning of the word contemporary is "living, occurring or existing at the same period of time", but due to a gross lack of communication between the arts community and lay groups, it connotes "that there abstract stuff" or a blob of the unknown. Relative to painting styles, many individuals prefer to remain contemporary only up to and including the late nineteenth century.

The 1850's and 1860's:

Academic Painting was, in effect, a series of historical works. The subject created a reason for the format and the grasp of space. Occasionally, satire was used, however it was followed by Realism, a viewpoint that seemed to now be replaced by the camera. Painting became polarized with Neo-classicism on one extreme and Romanticism and Neo-Romanticism on the other.

Academic Painting was the style supported by the official Salons of painting. Salons fought the trends of both Realism, as being of real people, and Impressionism as being of artistic interpretation. The prevailing Salon belief was that "flaws were not to be found" in painting. They only perceived of the styles shown by Realism and Impressionism as being flawed. Within the Academic Painting scenarios, art is controlled not by the painter who is expressing him or her self, but rather by a minority of individuals. In the past it was either governments or the institutions of higher learning that sanctioned this power over the arts. It was this hierarchy that appointed the power of critic and formal judgment. The Barbizon School created a partial acceptance of the painting of landscapes. Throughout this period, they were both with and without the depiction of peasants and their labours. Unfortunately the scenes were considered trivial as compared to the Academic School's chosen historical works. They were a group of landscape painters who gathered in 1830 in the small village of Barbizon, France. It is a reaction against the Classical Italianate landscapes and other non-fresh sentimental works of the past. During the prior two hundred years other oil painters had portrayed farm workers, however these new works were paintings of landscape, revealing an appreciation of nature's beauty as separate from individuals. In the 1550's the images of individuals were not seen as real people, they only served as allegories.

Closely following, in the 1560's, ceramic plate scenes had depicted normal hunting, fishing or harvesting scenes; nevertheless this was done in reference to the supply of food for the decorative plates and were not a part of this new thought. Long before the Barbizon Movement, a 1632 painting shows musical instruments being played – double bass, lute, violin, flute and harpsichord – and also depicts working class people. The occupations of the individuals are still shown by their dress alone, as being from the aristocracy. The furnishings or surroundings shown are of a lower class, usually that of the artist. To immediately follow were three brothers who were rehabilitated to the public by the art historians and critics of France and of the twentieth century, as they attained a new popularity.

As the focus of the Barbizon Movement drew attention to them, it became obvious that Antoine, Louis and Mathieu Le Nain were French painters who also had painted peasants for their own individuality. They painted in such a way that the painting became more than a mere anecdote or a quest for that which might be simply "pretty". The work of the brothers was approximately two hundred years prior to the Barbizon School. However as a subject the peasant farmers were still considered invisible in art by the mainstream population of culture consumers.

It was the Barbizon group of painters that then led the way for the Impressionists. Both groups painted outdoors. This style of landscape work being both dominant and most relevant, would evolve at later dates and in other countries, over the next one hundred years.

As a later example, this quest would evolve for the painters of the Canadian Group of Seven. As a group they shared a desire, to show the rustic beauty of the landscape of Canada in a style directly related to the subject matter. By way of their knowledge of European Art, they could set aside the Classical, and the Romantic. More importantly, they could ignore the European Salons and the Royal Canadian Academy of Arts, which in their day represented a very different standard of excellence compared to their more modern art. Because of this evolution, the Group of Seven would also move on to that which was uniquely their own.

The previous focus on perspective was set aside in some of the new styles of painting. Broken and free brush strokes were now being used as a specific effect. Brush strokes unrelated to Academic Painting were what the next thirty years of change would be all about. The brush strokes were described as broad, or generous, or sensual, or with luxuriant consistency. Flat colours of these broad, brush strokes were also often subtly incorporated, without any claim to convey perspective or depth of subject. By painting outdoors in this fashion of using rapidly brushed figures, replicating the changing light over several hours could be achieved. The tradition of using allegorical figures was now set aside. Contrasts between shade and light became more important than subject. For many painters the new freedom meant darker tones, heavily loaded brush marks creating heavy chiaroscuro – and even a purposeful deformity of the figure. Paintings of water with fragmented and quivering brushstrokes gave a blurred sense of a transient and fleeting natural look, and of a quick impression, whether they were seascapes or small ponds.

The initial works of the Impressionists were done outdoors. This technique of capturing the quickly passing moment with an extremely fast method of applying the paint to the canvas proved to be very compatible to their approach. Skin tones were now varied by patches of greens, blues, and purples, as part of the quest for capturing the ultimate light and sun. Geometrical structure was being addressed by the compositions. Horizontal lines with diagonal intersections and fragmented brush strokes were used, along with the subtle and innumerable variations in the atmosphere of the sky and the light.

There existed a great concern for the outlines of construction and a firm painting structure. In later works and within indoor works, composition was also paramount, with paintings now appearing in monochromatic themes as a study. Even in many Still Life compositions, form was now being experimented with.

The 1870's:

The first Impressionist exhibition was organized in Paris, France, in 1874, ade up from works rejected by the official Art Salon to the World Fair. Texture in painting had become more important. The modern life of the painter was now considered a legitimate subject. The capturing of a moment in time became the nature of painting. It was the impression that was paramount – thus "Impression-ism". Paint was often applied by moving the hand in either a spotting or plastering movement. This gave a texture and a unique quality to the landscape work. Often this effect was created by a palette knife in lieu of a brush. Silhouettes became more shapeless, allowing the viewer to interpret the actual subjects.

The challenge of the artist was that all artistic works were all meant to create and communicate the feelings of the artist. In that quest, the final outcome of the painting was meant to be distortion. A group calling themselves the Pre-Raphaelites had been formed in London, England in 1848. They were responding to the obvious evolution of art that was now taking place, and its consistent use of abstraction. Their quest was to return to the subjects, the purity and the techniques of the Masters, in a time prior to that of Raphael, the great Italian painter.

The 1880's:

The Impressionist painters were now an accepted group. They worked to capture the infinite variations of light and atmosphere on their subjects. To emphasize this, they often presented new subject matter, and even works in artificial light became part of their art. Impressionism is probably the most often used word in painting, and as such suffers irregularities of meaning. It is a term applied to the art that derived from the style of Naturalism, which aimed to analyze and record the exact value and colour of what the eye sees.

Theoretically, in Impressionism, the artist is concerned with the rendering of light playing over surfaces – without regard for the weights, tensions and volumes of forms, or of their linear contour. Feeling and content is subordinated to the perceptual study of light – its vibration, refraction and reflection – along with its composition of pure hues, and of warm and cool colours. The ultimate goal of Impressionism is to paint only the visual experience, rather than that which the mind knows. Detail is sacrificed to the overall impact, and a technique was developed where the artist would put down patches of pure colour – spontaneously, while in the presence of the motif or subject. By definition, this excludes the traditional prolonged study and compositional planning so long integral to the development of the painting. Nudes were now most often painted as if there was no audience. They were shown in their normal and daily environment.

A contrasting style of painting was developed, using randomly coloured stripes applied with energetic brushstrokes. Pure expression was the important goal. The fact that pure colour tone in itself signified a certain idea of closeness or distance was introduced.

This manner of painting led the way for the Fauves and the Expressionists. The last Impressionist Exhibition of 1886 marked the decline of the movement. Most artists who had been involved were now distanced from the style.

Neo-Impressionism (including Pointillism) had replaced it as a popular style. Neo-Impressionism was a more systemized development of Impressionism, and it followed the physical laws of light and colour combinations. It used a precise technique with organized dots of pure related colour. This is also called Divisionism or Pointillism, depending on technique; and by its use optical mixtures of a more brilliant colour is obtained. By playing on optical perception, the use of pixelated mixtures creates a more brilliant colour.

Divisionism was a later exploration of communication, which used larger staccato patches of non-objective colour. The Neo-Impressionists are also more concerned with the forms and compositional structure of the painting, than the more spontaneous Impressionists. One solution for the fading forms and de-structured compositions that had resulted from Impressionism evolved into the Pointillist technique.

The Pointillists used small brush marks of pure colour. By the middle of the decade, larger (often square) strokes were being used, and the works were becoming more spontaneous, expressive and lyrical. An art based on optical studies and the scientific theories of colour and light, is contrary to most perceptions of the spirit of art. The thought of using a consistent logic, in much the same way as an engineer would work from a blueprint, was very much in contrast to what most would consider the typical painter's methodology. The technique was set aside by many of the group, as it simply required too much time.

Paintings were next done with flowing brush-marks. Other techniques such as leaving parts of the bare canvas showing through were used for effect. For many painters, any illusion of seeking photographic representation was also set aside. This was the era of Post-Impressionism. In landscape, the colour planes were often without contours or exhibited vanishing lines.

In both portraiture and in representations of the nude, the body was defined with multiple facets and with the simplification of forms and masses. Nature was considered a synthesis of the cylinder, the sphere and the cone. The forms were reduced, in this way, to geometrical terms. By this handling of the pictorial space, the major art movements which would mark the beginning of the twentieth century were heralded.

Symbolism was emerging – with its presentation of feelings, dreams and imagination. As both a literary movement and an art movement, in England it became linked with the Pre-Raphaelite group that had preferred the antiquated style. The goal of the Symbolist movement was to paint the lines, the forms, the general colours – and anything else significant to the identity of the object. This goal dictated the addition of many partial symbols that could substantiate the general object, along with any other significant elements that were also to be exaggerated.

Despite the invention of photography in the mid-nineteenth century, the importance and prestige of having a portrait done in oil remained unchanged. Realism was often combined with Impressionism with great skill. The artists of the day could combine the heightened colour and sense of light of the Impressionists with the feeling for weight and detail from the old Masters. As one of the Impressionists, Cézanne had gone on to break up and fragment his forms, and he had then rearranged them in a fashion that at first seemed arbitrary. Angles and rectangles were patterned across the surface of the picture. This style would have much to do with all that was to be analytical in art, for the next century. The complexity of Cézanne's vision was not only being understood, but was also being experimented with by others. His ability to resolve conflicts between solidity and transparency, between form and anxiety, were now – more than ever – being addressed by the compositions of this era.

Geometrical structure now constituted a way of looking at painting. This use of line, the curve, and the observation of movement as used by the Impressionists, was to become a part of the Art Nouveau movement, which would follow in the next decade.

Rotating disks had been developed in Scotland such that optical mixtures of colours could be studied. In 1879 a book was published specifically for artists. It included calculations on the luminosity of optical mixtures and values of light. Various colour systems had now been developed. The two most accepted systems were both three-dimensional in form. One was based on twenty-four hues around an equator of solid colour. The intensity is the greatest at the outer edge and it decreases as it approaches the axis. The colour value is lightest at the top and darkest at the bottom.

The second system consists of five intermediate hues with reference to a commonly used circle, which is made up of gradually intensified colours. These are placed in a colour circle at a position of five in the three dimensional range of values of ten, running from white at the bottom. Intensity or chroma increases as it goes out from the neutral axis. The steps or intervals in this system are based on the eye, rather than the former photometric measurement. Colour systems have since been simplified to become colour wheels of two dimensional presentations. These systems of colour analysis, in two-dimensional form, predicated the quest for modern art.

The 1890's:

Post-Impressionism was the logical evolution of Impressionism. In turn, it developed into two branches. One stressed the emotional aspect of painting (Expressionism), while the other emphasized a return to formal structure, which would evolve into Cubism. Metaphors were used consistently in a new and modern sense. References to the Classical world were now all but extinct. The quest was now towards interpreting the greatest mysteries, with a focus on such concepts as life and death. The belief was that to create a new art, the artist had to turn inward. In an attempt to show the importance and the existence of the artist's internal and mental worlds, narrative paintings – often full of ambiguity – were composed. The presentation of life, mental turbulence, destiny, eroticism, and any other such meditations were now considered ideal, as paintings had become more intellectual than in any other time.

The decades that followed produced movements that crossed borders and cultures, even though in many cases, these consisted of only small groups of people. Very often, manifestos were written and sworn to, as unwaveringly as any creed. As strict as many of their manifestos were, deviations from these would often follow, with these changes often being extreme - in direct proportion to the outrageousness of the original fiat.

Expressionism was to follow. In order to better contemplate their use of form and colour, many painters returned to the studio. Expressionism was a stylistic development evolving from the aspect of Post Impressionism, which concerned itself with emotional identification in the expression of feelings, especially those that might be negative or unhappy. This reaction of the artist to life is expressed with tensions, distortions, and contrasts in form, space and colour. Brushwork is usually turbulent and instinctive, and reflects with emphasis on the subjective.

Cloisonnism with its flat colours – often outlined with dark contours – was yet another form of experimentation during this era. Coloured hatching strokes were used and then symbols were added. This style of painting derived its name from cloisonné enameling, a method of filling in metal-outlined areas with enamel. The painting style consists of flat decorative areas of colour, which are strongly outlined or cut out and pasted on. It evolved from an attempt to synthesize the visible world – with the patches of expression being symbolic of the attempt to fragment it for analysis.

The Symbolists did not paint things, but rather, the idea of things beyond what was being shown. By this perception, the logic of all that we see is at the service of all those fantasies which we don't see. Themes from mainline religions as well as demonology were also incorporated. Artistic concerns for contemporary life, love and death were often combined. When combining this style with other related styles the work may be called Synthetism. These esoteric, beautifully evocative delicacies explored in paint at the turn of the century would later evolve into an art abstracted from reality.

The Nabis were a faction of artists who called themselves a group; however, the group lasted for only a few years as each member set out to experiment in other of the many styles that were now evolving. The group's 'official' style was without relief or shading and was related to two-dimensional decoration. Their landscapes were very near to being abstract. Perspective was abolished and random flat colours gave the effect of removing all naturalistic characteristics. Although pure abstraction did not yet exist, for these painters, a vague subject matter was only inferred. Nature served as a subject of inspiration only, with the painter conveying his impression through colour equivalents. The painting was essentially a flat surface covered with colours assembled in a certain order. The Nabis believed that for every emotion and for every human thought, a purely decorative and beautiful equivalent exists. Their beliefs foreshadowed the major pictorial movements of both Cubism and Non-Objective Art.

Art Nouveau was a decorative curvilinear style based on the ornamental forms of nature. The movement originated in Belgium in the early 1890's. These artists were associated with, or re-named, Les Vigt in Belgium, Sezessionists in Austria and in Berlin, Jugendstil throughout the rest of Germany, and Stile Liberty in Italy. The term Jugendstil was from the word Jungend, which means youth.

1900 to 1910:

In England, The Camden Town Group was formed, retaining the influences of the Post-Impressionists. In 1913, they became The London Group. The stage was now also set elsewhere for the riotous colours of Fauvism. Painting was attempting to create a new reality. Fauvism had evolved as a rebellion against both Academic Art and Impressionism.

Les Fauves means wild beasts or wildcats in French. Their work employs complementary but pure and irrational colours. It shows flattened spaces and simplified design, with examples such as a green horse or a blue cow. Artistic temperament was integrated into this display of the infidelities of nature, highlighted by human values expressed in colour. "Fauvism" describing this movement is not really accurate. Instead of portraying nature like wild beasts, the Fauves painted pictures of luscious and often luxurious decoration, with detailed compositions that were the result of much thought. They created their own freedom to paint in erotic and sensuous colours and their palette included vivid reds and pinks; these would often be silhouetted against turquoise – or, upon occasion, against an extremely elaborately embellished background.

In English, Die Brücke means The Bridge. This movement was a successful attempt by German painters whose work derived from the French school of Fauvism. Attempting to work across borders, these were the same artists who would later help define Expressionism. Die

Brücke works examined the effects of the elements, and also took into account the new and changing, if not decadent, lifestyles that surrounded them. The quest was for communication in form, contour and composition, with colour often secondary. The art of this period frequently delved into a disembodied, spiritual universe, which would later evolve into Surrealism.

The role of Art Dealers was increasing. The patrons of the arts were the newly rich, and they constantly searched for the ideal upcoming young artist. Members of Die Brücke helped to fill this demand. In German art, the political agitation communicated by earlier Expressionistic work was being transformed into a more sober social criticism, characterized by Realism and related to the developing goals of Socialistic Realism. With a return to natural forms, politically presented, their works had been called Neue Sachlichkeit, a name which, when these works were later shown in New York, was translated as The New Objectivism.

The exhibit was shown as a planned reaction against both Post Impressionism and Expressionism Numerous art manifestos would come about over the next few years with many new groups. It became a scenario where artists could choose a particular style, and apply it on a work-by-work basis. As a result, each piece could be presented according to how the artist perceived their goals might be best achieved.

Cubism evolved as an attempt to solve the problems involved in correlating the relationships between two-dimensional space, with the illusion of three-dimensional form. Fundamentally figurative, Cubism attempted to synthesize everything visible into being a cylinder, a sphere or a cone. This evolved purely as an exploration of the relationships between shapes and space. One result of this quest was a palette that was often reduced to muted tones of gray, brown, and white. All of this combined to create a non-imitative art that permitted viewers new insights into the nature of reality.

Cubism also deals with structural qualities in which objects are broken into small facets or planes as Analytical Cubism. This requires analysis of both form and volume. The form is decomposed, simplified to geometric shape and reassembled from multiple points of view in an abstractly organized space. With the addition of increased spontaneity or with the arbitrary building up of objects through flat shapes (often times adding Collage), came the name, Synthetic Cubism.

Cubism would in turn lead to such movements as Constructivism and Futurism. With that came a sense of permanence regarding all manifestations of two-dimensional form but painting was still adhering to long established themes. These themes included park-like settings, architectural edifices, or specific indoor space. But all of this was about to change: line, space – and above all, colour – would soon lead an autonomous existence, freed from the traditional demands of representation.

Expression was now by means of line alone – or, as would later evolve – by colour alone.

The 1910's:

Der Blaue Reiter, a German group, used a great contemporary painting of a blue horse as their icon. Their abstractions carried forward the traditions of both Expressionism and Fauvism. During their later years, they moved towards an almost complete rejection of representational form. Using bold and strident colours, their later works often showed many semi-abstract symbols of either detailed or inferred items.

Futurism in painting was originally a derivative of Cubism. As such it revealed a belief in the artistic superiority of industrialism and the machine. The belief was that the glorification of man had been sacrificed to machines and that it now needed to be communicated with art. This dynamic and strident movement utilized techniques similar to those used in stroboscopic photography – in an attempt to render effects of speed and motion. Images were often the reenactment of the many varying positions in a stop-motion photograph. Futurism could be distinguished from Cubism by its use of dynamic lines and intense colour. By using separate two-dimensional planes to present multiple appearances of an object in motion, it created a simultaneity of vision. In effect, they were attempting to make a cult of technology as a celebration of modern life.

England saw the emergence of Vorticism. This movement held to many of the concepts of Futurism – but without its political element. In conforming to Victorian ideals, it attempted to show the inventors of modern machines as visionaries. As an art movement, Vorticism failed.

Orphic Cubism (or Orphism) was a development of Cubism in which the spectrum colours of Fauvism were used in large contrasting patches - as a colourist technique against the rather more dull Cubic paintings. Orphism saw the forms abstracted to a secondary role. It employed motion, staccato forms of colour, and volume, towards a grand theme of relating man to modern technology in a contemporary and structured order.

Suprematism was an abstract geometric form of Cubism which originated in Russia. Newly created forms were to represent absolutes – the realities of space, motion, and time that we cannot see but that we experience and know. It attempted to become both an artistic and a spiritual adventure for the painter. It failed. In Suprematist compositions, art was liberated from the weight of the object. The resulting effect signified the supremacy of pure feeling and perception. The reason their works represented no specific objects followed from their belief that only by being without subject could their works penetrate the essence of creation. Such were the contortions of their philosophical gymnastics.

Simultaneism was a later form of Orphic Cubism distinguished by a contrast of colours. It is a term which defines: presenting superimposed images in the same painting, describing an object's various aspects, or showing objects from various points of view.

Collage is a methodology of incorporating objects, initially used by the Cubists. It is the pasting of any object – often a part of a newspaper page, or a current magazine – onto the surface of a work. The paint around the surface of the collage then becomes an integral part of the communication. Including actual things from the world around us, and incorporating them as part of the canvas, addresses the philosophical question about the relationship between illusion and reality. With the invention of collage, it became permissible to introduce all kinds of elements into the canvas. Sculpture and painting would now have a different relationship with each other, as the lines defining each had now changed. The doors had been opened so that exciting hybrids – part sculpture and part two dimensional painting – could now be created.

The Found Object was also called The Ready-Made Object. More relevant to sculptural exhibits than painting, it created the freedom of adding everyday objects. This evolved into the object becoming the entire work of art – a validation based upon the fact that it had been given a title, which thus put it into a new context. It was not just a simple and passing iconoclastic gesture; rather, it marked an important, irreversible, and visible step in the history and evolution of art.

Metaphysical Painting contains dreamlike overtones in what may at first seem to be a naïve interpretation of life. Mystery, a melancholy isolation, and a foreboding sense of the unreal are present in changing perspectives. These paintings often include long, illogical shadows and strangely-related objects. Geometric forms are dominant along with contrasts of portraying antique objects within a modern world. The works were most often painted in the detailed manner of Surrealism, which in this case is also similar to the perfection of the art of the Renaissance. Women were generally portrayed in an erotic or sexual context.

Dada is the only movement that may be considered anti-rational and anti-aesthetic. It was equally opposed to the pathos of Expressionism, the patriotic stance of Futurism and the sense of structure in Cubism. Unfortunately, by not evolving, it became a type of Nihilism. The Dada doctrine was not so much a style in painting as a movement that was motivated by disillusionment, cynicism, and disgust with the social values of the time. Collage and Montage were common to many Dada works; unfortunately, good painting wasn't. Although not prone to wanting to be part of the art scene in which it existed, it did anticipate Surrealism – both with its choice of unique subject matter as well as with its evident desire to outrage, shock or generally exasperate its viewers. Metaphors and subconscious associations were other integrated concepts that linked Dada with Surrealism. Many of these attitudes would re-emerge later in Pop Art, Psychedelic Art and Happenings as a form of non-conventionalism.

Nihilism is a belief that nothing should change, thus initiating a non-creative environment. To be against all contemporary art movements, is by a definition being nihilist - as in the expression: "I don't want art information, I know what I like."

The 1920's:

Out of all of this came The Group of Seven on our "local" Canadian scene. They are the most well known of Canadian painters: Frederick Varley, Frank Carmichael, A. Y. Jackson, Lawren Harris, Frank Johnston, Arthur Lismer, and J. E. H. MacDonald. Tom Thomson is often considered to be one of the group, due to his having inspired them in their search for a distinctive Canadian style, especially in landscape. A. J. Casson joined the group in 1926. When listed beside the European heavyweights they may seem rather unimportant. However, to many of us, they established the ultimate rules for how paintings depicting our rugged country needed to evoke a landscape that was much different from that of Europe.

Over the next ten years, throughout the Western World, there would be a return to naturalism and advocacy of an art based on national experience rather than on the formal values of abstraction. Almost all of the northern European countries were reacting positively to an idea known as Regionalism – that is, avoiding foreign influences and expressing the true spirit of the land. It was also a response to the political and economic realities of the Depression era.

In Canada, the style of The Group of Seven was one of simplified forms which, on occasion, borrowed the colours of Fauvism. Linear contours of landscape were occasionally inspired by Art Nouveau. During their heyday, it was a very welcome message to any type of Canadian culture consumer, that Canada could now offer its own valid style of modern art. The Group's last exposition was in 1931, after which the further new trends of European Art became their influence and focus.

Constructivism was a movement involving architectural theories that were also related to Cubism. Its practitioners used a variety of materials in geometrical and mathematical interrelationships. Their use of three-dimensional objects surpassed the former use of material as Collage - often to the point where the work would become a wall relief or sculpture in form.

Neo-Plasticism was a movement that resulted from the conceptualizing of architecture. Simple and geometric in style, it was applied to other forms of design besides painting, mainly through association with the De Styl movement. It lends itself to theories of colour relationships and their evocation of dimension and depth. Surface planes, horizontal and vertical lines, colour plates of pure colour, including white and black – all related to theories common to interior design and architecture.

Purism was the name given to a movement, almost synonymous to Constructivism, which also derived from Cubism. It emphasized precision, clarity, and the impersonal technological and mechanical influences of modern life. The movement's artistic works had much less influence than the writings that accompanied them.

Geometric Abstraction is a nonrepresentational style of painting that uses two-dimensional geometric shapes, rather than shapes of perspective.

Where Modern Art can be seen as a continuous series of reductions, perspective was the element which was now being set aside. There was more concentration on the aspects of formal composition, using shapes such as triangles, squares, rectangles and circles.

De Styl (Dutch for "The Style") was a movement originating in Holland that applied the principle of geometric abstraction to both the fine and applied arts. De Styl theories had been incorporated into the principles advocated by the Bauhaus Group in Germany. These principles again dealt with the relativity of colour relationships, with the optical mutations of form, with the interaction of colour and light in space, and with the optical and psychological meanings of illusion.

Surrealism is a broad movement in literature and art that aimed to remove rationality from the creative process, and to replace it with subconscious manifestations, especially those expounded by Freud. The dogmatic belief in the superior reality of associations, the supremacy of subconscious impulse and the "omnipotence of the dream" were basic to the Surrealists as a way of looking at life. Bold choices of subject matter – including fetishes, sexual fantasies, and dream images – were executed with extreme technical virtuosity. They were often accomplished with great detail, using thin glazes in the Renaissance tradition. Surrealism developed into two general styles. One uses meticulous classic techniques of detail to naturalistically illustrate the visions and dreams. The other is a non-figurative, spontaneous and impulsive style, which was later called Abstract Surrealism or Action Painting.

During this period, the Central Committee of the Soviet Union officially condemned all forms of abstraction in art. In Mexico, large murals with vast compositions were painted to dictate a general understanding of the history of the country and to further the ambitions of the socialistic government. In both countries, as a non-elitist art, it was hoped that such historically representative work would help bring about a transition from a decrepit society to a new order. The political value to a largely illiterate mass, within their revolutionary struggle, was parallel to the use of stained glass windows, with their religious messages, during the Middle Ages in Europe. The two movements were known in general as Socialistic Realism. The style of the murals became known as purely Mexican, however, the intent was indirectly related to the Soviet process of eliminating freedom in art.

The 1930's:

Fantastic Art is found in the art of all periods. It is characterized by the imaginative and the enigmatic, and it includes the anti-rational works of Dada and the creative works of Surrealism. During the 1930's in Europe, great art works commemorating bombing, destruction, and war in general were painted in many contemporary styles. Their "reason for being" was that they represented symbols of hope. These were works of premonition, prior to yet another world war.

Pure Abstraction is by definition: Non-representational, Non-figurative, or Non-objective Art, as it does not depict any recognizable visual object. The term usually pertains to geometric shapes, but is sometimes applied to embryonic forms or even amorphous creations.

Abstract Expressionism is a movement in abstract art that relies on a spontaneous intuitive approach to painting and sculpture, with emphasis on the act of painting rather than the result. An affirmation of the physical activity in creating a painting (often resulting in a dramatization of the accidentals of drip, dribble and splash), is also referred to as Action Painting.

Abstraction is a relative term, actually present in all painting. Abstraction as an action does not necessarily make the object painted recognizable (or, for that matter, unrecognizable); rather it is an evocation of an ambience, a sensation or an idea. The abstract elements of line, shape, colour and space are used in representing any recognizable concrete object so that it may be re-created on a two dimensional surface, and not rendered with actual texture or three-dimensionally. According to this line of thought, colour, line, shape, space and light – all pictorial elements – no longer have recourse to the known world, as the artist communicates his most inner feelings directly onto the canvas. It is a world of pure colour relationships, with the only deep emotional significance being colour and its rhythms.

Abstract Expressionism is where colour alone becomes both form and subject.

The 1940's:

Hard Edge Painting is a term used to describe a style of abstract painting characterized by a precise geometrical division of planes, which often consist of pure colours. It is antithesis to the "lost-and-found" or blended contours of a more painterly approach. Hard Edge is in the tradition of the De Styl movement and its principles of abstract geometric design. In general, this was an era with war artists working at or near the front lines.

During the entire decade, themes of war and its aftermath concerned the majority of artists, most of whom were now painting in their personally chosen styles. The human situation, rather than formal structure, was the motivation and object of their art - and it would be the dominant focus of this decade.

The 1950's:

Optical Painting (often called Op Art) is a form of geometric painting that uses a variety of visual phenomena and optical illusions. Principles, which are important to optical painting, include: simultaneous contrast, after image, interpenetration of shape and volume, plotted grids and colour displacement with the ambiguity of spatial relationships. The interaction of colours is meant to attack the eye, producing an immediate physiological sensation. The carefully manipulated colour surface stimulates the optic nerve and activates vision. An adjustment of the eye is demanded.

Metapolymorphic Painting was a name given – for its commercial value – to the type of Optical Painting in which the picture changes according to how the viewer changes his own position. This novel effect is obtained by employing various three-dimensional painting techniques, such as constructing a modified Venetian blind on the painting's surface, or an offset grille or even mirrors.

Tachism is a style in which colour is applied in splotches or blots of colour. "Tache" is French for marks, stains or splashes. These taches are often placed on the canvas spontaneously and by chance; however, planned composition may be a part of the process. Dynamic strokes of brush and palette knife are used to create texture and often a deluge of colour. Pigments are vigorously stacked on top of each other to build a dense, tactile surface over the entire canvas. These powerful rhythms of multidirectional strokes and daubs of colours, are recording the artist's impulses during creation.

The 1960's:

Pop Art, also called New Realism, was the name given to a faddish anti- traditional glorification of mass culture. It was commercially promoted and merchandized, but paradoxically, it revealed the pretence that existed within even its own presentation of mass media advertising, becoming almost a send-up of itself.

Gagart, which inevitably followed, is a term for Pop Art created entirely for the purposes of being an art gag.

Psychedelic Art is a projected mélange of painting, photography, animated electronics, and geometric forms. The artist aimed to produce the hallucinatory effects and so-called perceptions that LSD and other psychedelic drugs could create. Contrary to perception, the creation did not involve using drugs. The art style was part of the fashion of the time, an era of undue exaggeration.

Synchromism is a colourful and geometrically abstract development of Cubism often used by the Paris Group of Painters. A significant resurgence in Mural Painting now occurred. Many artists rejected the idea of making collectible art objects for a consumer society. Most painted in the style of Realism, the murals usually depicted community based interests and subjects. The trend to commission artists to bring visual appeal to the urban environment had now spread throughout Europe.

Primitivism represents the confluence between modern art and the paintings and objects of primitive civilizations. It came into style at the turn of the twentieth century and now, one hundred years later, it seems again to be one of the most popular of mannerisms. Most often used within a stylized approach to painting groups of people, it is easy to forget that Aboriginal art was its root. Many landscape works that seem devoid of atmosphere, paintings that contain such devices as unrealistic skies or unnatural perspective, may be satisfactory to the viewer, as long as they are under the caption of being "Primitive". "Tourist Art" is another classification that can be perceived by a viewer. In general, such works are painted by a much lesser quality of artist – someone who is required to merely be a technician. The painting is then not obliged to be of any "art movement", nor is the artist required to have mastered his or her craft. However, criticism has always been a difficult-to-determine calibration of quality. In the end, many contest that art can only be judged pleasing, or not, by the subjective eye of its viewer. Primitivism is a specific example of the process.

The Paris School of Painters was a group who were active in Paris in the late Middle Ages and who painted in the style of the "Illuminators," using candlelight reflections within their paintings.

The second group to use the term were some of the Expressionists who lived in the artistic centre – the Montparnasse or the Montmartre areas – of Paris. The name Paris School of Painters, as a term, has now lost any reference to a single group of painters and now refers to any contemporary group centred in Paris, France. It refers to an international sharing of ideas and in the sixties we enjoyed being referred to as a part of this group. However, we were well aware that New York had by then replaced Paris as the world capital of contemporary art.

CHRONOLOGY OF CONTEMPORARY ART

Classical Art
Neo-Classicism
Romanticism
Neo Romanticism,
Neo-Humanistic
The Barbizon School 1830
Pre-Raphaelites 1848
The Realists 1855
Naturalism Academic Painting

The 1870's

Impressionism 1874
Mannerism

The 1880's

Neo-Impressionism 1885
Divisionism or Pointillism
Symbolism
Post-Impressionism

The 1890's

> Expressionism
> Cloisonnism
> Symbolism
> The Nabis
> Art Nouveau,
> Les Vigt (in Belgium),
> Sezessionists
> Jugendstil (in Germany),
> Stile Liberty (in Italy)

1900 to 1910

> Camden Town Group,
> London Group
> Fauvism
> Die Brücke (The Bridge)
> Neue Sachlichkeit (New Objectivism)
> Cubism
> Analytical Cubism
> Synthetic Cubism

The 1910's

> Der Blaue Reiter 1911
> Futurism Vorticism (in England)
> Orphic Cubism (Orphism) 1913
> Suprematism
> Simultaneism 1916
> Hybrids of Collage
> The Found Object (A Ready-Made)
> Metaphysical Painting (Pittura Metafisica)
> Dada

The 1920's

        The Group of Seven
        Constructivism
        Neo-Plasticism
        Purism
        Geometric Abstraction
        De Styl (in Holland)
        The Bauhaus Group (in Germany)
        Surrealism 1924
        Abstract Surrealism or Action Painting
        Socialistic Realism

The 1930's

        Fantastic Art
        Pure Abstraction (Non-representational, Non-figurative, Non-objective)
        Abstract Expressionism

The 1940's

        Hard Edge Painting

The 1950's

        Optical Art (Op Art)
        Metapolymorphic Painting)
        Tachism

The 1960's

        Pop Art (New Realism)
        Gagart
        Psychedelic Art
        Synchromism
        Primitivism

Throughout history every artist has been moved by the beauty of line, colour, and each special relationship for their own sake - and not by what they represent. The last century of the evolution of painterly expression, has been relative to established colour implying:

(1) the reduction of natural colour to primary colour,

(2) the reduction of colour to flatness and

(3) the enclosure of colour as rectangular or circular planes with resolved rhythmic unity.

Almost all the art movements of the last one hundred years relate to this generalized description.

By its nature this book cannot be a detailed explanation of art, and by its objective it can only be a summary. The ultimate goal in writing is always communication – not overdoing the literary gymnastics and, of course, not creating confusion. However, communicating a basis for understanding art seems to require the use of these rather unique "executive summaries" for the reader. For many of the listed art movements substantial Manifestos and formal Theories were published under the signatures or authorship of the artists involved. In these instances, definitions of their art were very structured, and their goals were very precise – so they would not be merged or confused with other, similar movements.

Even the artists who were in cooperation with a particular group or school would often need to move onward. Frequently this meant a phase of disagreement, before they could proceed with pursuing their quests for the new and elusive line, texture or colour

In contrast, for many readers, this type of summary may be all that is required to enhance their personal enjoyment of painting. As an example, the same logic of using only summaries prevailed with the decision to not list the many movements which were simply offshoots, or part of a movement's natural evolution, such as Post-Cubism. One such movement, often called Tube-ism, where everything is reduced to basic geometric shapes such as a tube, represents a normal evolution of an art movement.

When searching for better mode of communication, it can be said that every movement has its own post-movement phase. The artist within a movement, by his or her very nature, is constantly searching for a better way. For example, many of the artists involved with Cubism would then go on to their own refinements of Cubism.

By this rationale, it can be seen that it would be redundant to list all of these post-movements within a short synopsis. Art movements were often so fleeting that one, which was dubbed Intimistism, held a grand total of two painters as its members (the Intimists). Both were well respected, however the need – or lack of need – to memorize such group names, is exemplified by its usual inclusion. The two were Edouard Vuillard and his lifelong friend, Pierre Bonnard. They were also members of a much larger, well-known group, the Nabis.

As colour retained its prominence as both form and subject, attempts were made to redefine some of the trends. Colour Field Painting and Post-Painterly Abstraction were two such attempts. These works displayed high-keyed colour, executed in open and often airy designs. Surely, these were attempts at repackaging existing philosophies and explanations of technique, while working in the hope of establishing yet another unique manifesto.

Through all of this remained the danger of a general public finally turning away from the art scene in frustration. Many of the movements listed were originally literary movements. Or inversely, as in Impressionism,

Realism and several others, the literary movements were derived from the paintings.

The painters' studios often served as salons for many poets, authors, and other artists. This sense of having a meeting place and being a part of a group with a common focus, provided both a sense of stability and purpose to the ever-fleeting philosophies. Defining a movement with a specific time frame is an unusual proclamation. The interpretation of when a movement existed is calibrated in more that one manner. The artist first pursued or developed the style with his or her approach

There is another time, often set off by as much as a decade - as when the critics may have declared a name to the style. The popularity of the movement may be at a third period. However in most cases, the time I have chosen to designate is aligned to the artist's quest – whether that pursuit occurred as an individual, or as part of a focused group. The vocabulary used within the art scene was always evolving. It has always included many of its own expressions, which themselves have often evolved to have multiple connotations. For this reason as well, many art movements are not listed.

Considering local processes of political thought, as well as regional and cultural differences, it is only the larger writings on history that can offer more detailed description. This then has been a general road map to help readers enjoy various styles in painting.

It is also the general map of knowledge that I use when I look at a blank canvas and must determine which type of painting I will be challenged by. It is this smorgasbord of available styles that confronts the painter each time he or she prepares to begin a work. And it is exactly that expansive palette offered by such an overview, which enhances the artist's quest.

EPILOGUE

No art book should be without a few select quotes:

"We must seek out those craftsman whose instinct guides them to whatever is lovely and gracious; so that our young men, dwelling in a wholesome climate, may drink in good from every quarter, whence, like a breeze bearing health from happy regions, some influence from noble works constantly falls upon eye and ear from childhood upward, and imperceptibly draws them into sympathy and harmony with the beauty of reason, whose impress they take." – Plato

"I am simply calling attention to the fact that fine art is the only teacher except torture." – George Bernard Shaw

"Art we have defined as mankind's effort to achieve integration with the basic forms of the physical universe and the organic rhythms of life." – Herbert Read

"The two most engaging powers of an artist are to make new things familiar, and familiar things new." – Frank Johnston

"In art, there is only one thing worthwhile and that is what cannot be explained." – George Braque

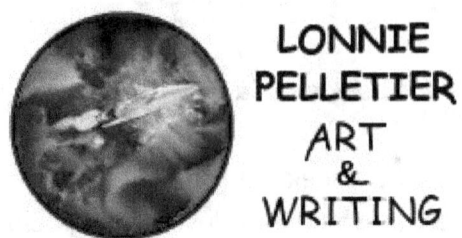

LONNIE PELLETIER ART & WRITING

Thank you for reading and contemplating both my book and my art. My art and writing may be viewed at:

http://LonPelletier.com

— Lon Pelletier